Where the forest murmurs, there is music, ancient, everlasting.

- Fiona McLeod

A man need not know how to name all the oaks or the moths...or tell time by the stars, in order to possess nature.

- Donald Peattie

He who observes beauty, contains it.

- Bernard Malamud

To most people, the first image brought to mind by the word "trail" is a lonely path in a quiet woods. These traditional trails can be walked alone, or perhaps with a partner or with treasured friends. Many Florida trails are just like that. They pass through quiet pine flatwoods, past cypress swamps, beside rivers, around marshes, and along beaches. These trails are places of solitude and peace of mind. This is where the soul of the real Florida can still be experienced.

But "trail" no longer necessarily means wilderness and wildlife. Urban trails have been created, a type of outdoor gym, where people of all ages bike, roller blade, or walk. Mom pushes a baby stroller while she jogs, and grandparents take their daily constitutional. Groups from bicycling and blading clubs flash past. Instead of offering solitude, these types of trails are often loud and crowded, and are sometimes located beside busy streets. The only people enjoying solitude are those wearing headphones.

Some of the traditional outdoor trails are found in parks created during the Great Depression by members of the Civilian Conservation Corps. Trails were greatly expanded during a period of growing ecological awareness in the 1960s and 1970s. The current expansion of trails is proceeding at a rapid pace, but not just to create employment, or because of a love of the outdoors and wild things. Instead it is driven mainly by volunteers seeking recreation, particularly bicyclists.

The definition of a trail has been greatly stretched. Portions of the Florida National Scenic Trail pass along roads. Some of the most popular bicycle trails are dirt or graded roads in wildlife management areas and on water management district lands.

This is still cause for celebration, because many wonderful places are now open for exploration. There is, in fact, a staggering number of natural places on public lands available for recreation, and a great many urban trails. There are several hundred places described in this book with well over 700 separate trails.

ORGANIZATION

How were locations selected for this book? The criterion is that the site must have trails at least three miles long. The focus is primarily on federal and state land. There has been no arbitrary or personal attempt to rate trails. Readers are encouraged to judge, based on the size of an area and the activities offered, whether it is suitable for them or not.

The trails are placed within four geographic regions: Northwest, North, Central, and South.

Within each region, trails are organized alphabetically by the land unit. When possible, directions are given from the nearest interstate.

Many county trails of three miles or more are included. Most county trails are short and used primarily by local residents. Some trails with less than three miles are included at the end of each region based on the sole criterion of pleasurable personal experience.

Addresses, phone numbers, and in some cases e-mail addresses of these sites can be found in Appendix A. It is always a good idea to obtain information and know current conditions before a visit. With very large areas, it is wise to obtain a map, often available free (or for a small charge) from the management agency.

Bicycle trails are generally off-road and require wide-tire mountain bikes unless noted as paved. Equestrian users would be wise to inquire in advance concerning water sources, stabling, and overnight camping.

When a location is described as multi-use, it means some part of it is open for all three uses (bicycling, hiking, and horseback riding). The trend is for new trails to be multi-use, in part to attract more revenues, while spending less for building and maintaining them. Multi-use does not necessarily mean that all trails are open for all uses, and it is best to check at the location concerning current allowed uses.

Directions to each location are in the text. Distances used are approximations.

There are areas in this book that could be considered worth driving across a continent to experience and others worth a brief day-trip. The Panhandle has more areas worth the longer trip than any other region of the state. These include the Apalachicola Bluffs and Ravines, Apalachicola National Forest, Blackwater River State Forest, Eglin Air Force Base, St. Josephs Peninsula and Torreya State Park.

A prominent characteristic of Northwest Florida is the presence of many rivers, some quite large, all with appealing views, including: the Apalachicola, Aucilla, Blackwater, Chipola, Econfina, Escambia, Shoal, and Yellow. Many of these rivers are premier canoe or kayak streams. There are also many smaller rivers and springs, including the world's most powerful spring, Wakulla Springs, located south of Tallahassee.

What are the typical sights? In addition to longleaf pine, the tree that perhaps most typifies both North and Northwest Florida is dogwood, with white blossoms standing out beneath pine forests, and titi which blooms beside swamps. Insect-eating pitcher plants are common in both regions. Perhaps the bird of most interest within the region is the red-cockaded woodpecker, because it is most easily seen within this area and also because of its endangered status. Another bird many people are eager to see is the swallow-tailed kite.

Geographically, this is a region with hills on the inland areas and sometimes towering sand dunes along the barrier islands. The Northwest is perhaps most amazing to Floridians from the south who can appreciate how different it is from the rest of the state.

For those riding bicycles or hiking, the Northwest has blessings and challenges. It is the most temperate of Florida's climate zones, with more cold days and longer fall and winter seasons. It also has the most ups and downs, which makes for strenuous exercise, whether pedaling up a grade or climbing down a cliff.

Opposite page: **cypress, both dead and alive, at Dead Lakes, a flooded elbow of the Chipola River.**

Above: **dogwood, a common flowering tree in Northwest and North Florida.**

APALACHICOLA BLUFFS AND RAVINES PRESERVE
(Liberty County, 6,265 acres, hiking)

A 3.5-mile, arduous, isolated hike, up and down ravines, is rewarded by the spectacular view of the Apalachicola River from cliffs approaching 200 feet in height. This sandhill ecosystem has extensive longleaf pine (sandhill is basically well-drained pinelands). There is great variation in plants and trees within the ravines.

From I-10, take SR-12 south 19.5 miles to Garden of Eden Road, 1 mile north of Bristol. There is a parking lot at the trailhead.

Managed by: the Nature Conservancy.

APALACHICOLA NATIONAL FOREST
(Franklin, Leon, Liberty, Wakulla counties, multi-use)

This enormous forest with two administrative divisions approaches 600,000 acres. The forest is divided by the Ochlockonee River into east and west districts.

While the forest often seems to be continuous flatwoods, with wiregrass and colorful wild flowers beneath, there is tremendous variety. Swamps range from peat bogs with insect-eating pitcher plants, to those dominated by hardwoods and titi. Some rivers are almost dry sand beds in times of drought, but become raging streams during heavy rainfalls. There are also rivers, like the Ochlockonee, that flow strongly year round, and the most powerful Florida river, the Apalachicola. One of Florida's two Styx rivers is found in this forest, as are the New and Sopchoppy rivers. The forest also includes extensive floodplain, marsh, and prairie.

In the east, a premier hike is the Leon Sinks Geological Area. The trail turns and meanders from one visually stunning sinkhole to another. In one, trees sprout from the walls. In another lies a pond. From a platform at the largest (the Big Dismal Sink) one can peer down into a mysterious, watery abyss.

The Florida Trail, maintained by the Florida Trail Association, traverses the forest in both the east and west sections. Because there are many forest roads, it is possible for teams of hikers to park one car ahead at a desired exit

ROAD DESIGNATIONS
CR =County Road
FR =Forest Road
SR =Florida State Road
US =United States Road
I is for interstate

spot, and leave another where the hike started. Another alternative is primitive camping along the way.

The Florida Trail in the east begins on US-319 in Medart and ends 32.6 miles later on FR-13 at Porter Lake Bridge. It passes through Bradwell Bay Wilderness, a wild, wet, swampy area, where bears are sometimes seen. The West Trail proceeds from Porter Lake to CR-12, 5 miles beyond Camel Lake, a total distance of 36.9 miles. Camel Lake is a Florida Trail loop.

The Mud Swamp/New River Wilderness is a large, isolated area with no designated trails. It is for those adventurous hikers who possess confidence and a compass.

As with other national forests, there are many camping opportunities, both primitive and less rugged. There are hundreds of miles of well maintained roads. A forest map is a must for exploration and can be obtained from either of the ranger districts. It is very helpful in locating the following trails.

TRAILS IN THE APALACHICOLA EAST
Bicycling: Munson Hill Bike Trail: 8.5-mile loop, accessed from the Tallahassee-St. Marks State Trail (see page 18). Bicycling is allowed on all forest roads.

Equestrian: allowed within the forest. The Vinzant Trail, a designated trail of 30.7 miles is 10 miles west of Tallahassee on SR-20. As with all areas allowing equestrian use in the state, proof of a current negative Coggins test is required.

Hiking: Bradwell Bay Wilderness, 7 miles. Florida Trail, 32.6 miles. Leon Sinks Geological Area, 4.8 miles.

TRAILS IN THE APALACHICOLA WEST
Bicycling: allowed on all forest roads.
Equestrian: horseback riding is allowed within the forest.
Hiking: Camel Lake, 9.4 miles. Florida Trail, 36.9 miles. Wright Lake Interpretive Trail, 5 miles.

Forest Location. This national forest is mostly south of Tallahassee, extending west to the Apalachicola River. It is roughly bordered in the north by SR-20, in the south by US-98, in the east by US-319, and in the west by SR-379. The ranger office in the east is on US-319 in Crawfordville. The ranger office in the west is on SR-20 in Bristol.

Opposite page, top left: the view from the Apalachicola Bluffs overlooking the Apalachicola River from a height of approximately 180 feet.

Opposite page, top, right: Hammock Sink in the Leon Sinks Geological Site, Apalachicola National Forest, one of a series of sinkholes found there.

Above, top: a hiker in the flatwoods approaching Bradwell Bay, Apalachicola National Forest.

Above: a pitcher plant bog in the Apalachicola National Forest.

Right: Econfina Creek flowing through Pitt Spring, a Northwest Florida Water Management District land with almost 3 miles of hiking and a walled spring for swimming.

THE FLORIDA TRAIL ASSOCIATION

Hiking trails in Florida might be few and far between without the efforts of this dedicated group. Volunteers have blazed trails, constructed boardwalks and bridges, and provided maintenance, often at their own expense. Regional chapters conduct work on trails, as well as workshops and camp-outs.

Just as the National Scenic Trail is an attempt to connect the entire US with footpaths, the Florida Trail Association seeks to do the same for Florida. While most segments are on public lands, some pass through private property where an association membership card in possession is required. In some cases, use of the private property requires advance permission through the state office.

Approximately 1,300 miles of trails are planned for Florida. Of this, perhaps 1,000 could be called complete. However, many sections presently on road rights-of-way are in transition, with hopes of placing the trails through natural areas. In addition to the main trail, a number of loop trails have been created.

Florida Trail segments are discussed throughout this book along with the public lands where they are located. Those that are not on public lands are in alphabetical order by region listed by the name assigned by the associaton. The state office address is in the Appendix. Through this office members can purchase high-quality, laminated maps for the trail sections.

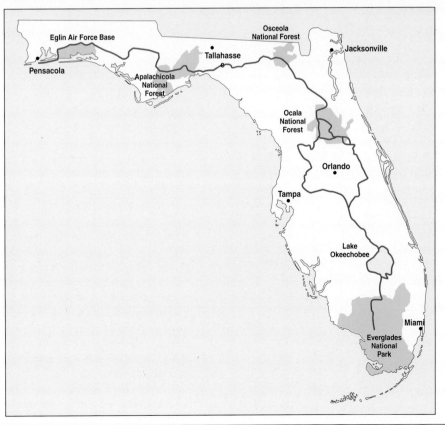

PC

APALACHICOLA RIVER WILDLIFE AND ENVIRONMENTAL AREA
(Franklin and Gulf counties, 55,000+ acres, multi-use)

Designated trails are being developed for use in 2001. Horseback riding is permitted. In addition, there are footpaths and good roads sufficient for bicycling. On the uplands are flatwoods, and in the floodplain there are cypress, as well as hardwoods like gum and tupelo (tupelo trees, with the help of bees, yield tupelo honey). Near Apalachicola Bay, there is saltmarsh. Four entrances lie south of Sumatra on the west side of SR-65, which parallels the Apalachicola River.

Managed by: Florida Fish and Wildlife Conservation Commission.

Above: the dark waters of the Aucilla River Sinks. The sinks are part of a channel through which the river flows underground.

AUCILLA WILDLIFE MANAGEMENT AREA
(Jefferson, Taylor, and Wakulla counties, 43,905 acres, multi-use).

This area used to total almost 80,000 acres, but in the year 2000, a separate, permit-only Flint Rock Wildlife Management Area was created on private land south of US-98. The Aucilla area open for use is north of US-98. However, the state is negotiating to buy two land units in Flint Rock and these will be added to the Aucilla. Major habitats in this area include pine flatwoods, floodplain, hardwood hammocks, marsh, river, and sinkholes.

Twenty miles of the Florida Trail are designated the Aucilla River Section. Smaller units include the Aucilla River, 7.1 miles, and the Aucilla Sinks, 4.4 miles. The Aucilla Sinks are a highlight of the Florida Trail. There, in a portion shaded by hardwoods, the dark waters of the Aucilla River run through an underground channel, visible as they appear and disappear in a series of sinkholes.

There are also over 40 miles of multi-use, improved and unimproved roads which are firm enough for good bicycling. While the area is open to equestrian use, there are a number of limitations. First, there is no parking area at present which is adequate to handle a horse trailer. Second, horses are not permitted on the Florida Trail or in Goose Pasture Campground. Third, there is no water setup.

The hiking trailheads are at SR-14 (SR-257A) north of US-98, and at the Aucilla River Bridge on US-98 to the west of Perry. A short cut to the sink area is as follows: from Newport, go 14 miles east on US-98, then turn north on Limestone Industries Road (PAL Hammock Road), then go west on Goose Pasture Road and proceed to the trail markers. Hike south to the sinks.

Managed by: Florida Fish and Wildlife Conservation Commission

BIG BEND WILDLIFE MANAGEMENT AREA
(Dixie and Taylor counties, 59,000+ acres, multi-use)

The "Big Bend" is the part of the Florida peninsula which "bends" westward toward the Panhandle. It is usually defined as the lands between the Apalachicola and Suwannee rivers.

The Big Bend Wildlife Management Area includes four separate units: Hickory Mound Unit, Jena, Spring Creek, and Tide Swamp. They are open for bicycling and hiking. In the year 2,000, there were only dirt and shell roads, and footpaths, but trails are planned. The washboard-like ride into Hickory Mound Unit is bone-jarring and hard on shock absorbers, despite periodic grading.

There are excellent roads around Hickory Mound for bicyclists who survive the auto ride. There are more than 45 miles of gravel or limestone roads in the area. The impoundment also has observation towers and borders vast areas of saltmarsh along the Gulf of Mexico. During the migratory seasons, birding is sensational. Two trails are being developed in Hickory Mound; one multi-use, one for hiking.

Two trails are in progress in the Tide Swamp Unit which also has 25 miles of roads that were once old logging trams. Spring Creek and Jena have over 30 miles of remote wooded roads leading to Gulf vistas. Scenic CR-361 parallels the coastal marsh through the Jena Unit.

Hickory Mound Unit and Spring Creek are south of US-98, 15 miles west of Perry. Tide Swamp is west of Cross City from US-19/98 along CR-51 and CR-351 to CR-357. Jena can be reached by either CR-361 or CR-357.

Managed by: Florida Fish and Wildlife Conservation Commission

Top, left: atamasco lilies bloom white and fade to pink.
Top, right: a yellow-fringed orchid.
Right: pitcher plants in Blackwater River State Forest.

WILDLIFE MANAGEMENT AREAS

The Florida Fish and Wildlife Conservation Commission is one arm of state government which manages areas with trails. While many of these lands have no designated trails, almost all have service roads, and some have their own trails or portions of the Florida Trail.

Most of these lands are managed for hunting. Some allow fishing. They can be on private or public land, or a mix of both. Many are water management district lands.

It is best to check during hunting season to make sure recreational access is allowed. Those who use hunt areas during season should invest in two items of clothing. Orange vests and "Elmer Fudd" hats are available from most sporting goods stores. Both stand out, the orange hat bobbing up and down through the forest as one walks. Many other colors, even white and red, can be confused with markings on game, such as deer or turkey.

Information on recreational use of wildlife management areas (including maps for over 100 areas) is on the internet (see Appendix). Printed regulations with maps can be obtained by mail. In general, most of the wildlife management areas are multi-use, but it is best to inquire in advance, particularly if taking a horse. There is an annual publication, the "Hunting Handbook & Regulations Summary," with a chart indicating what uses are allowed and if permits or fees are necessary.

WILDLIFE ALERT

Part of the duties of the Florida Fish and Wildlife Conservation Commission is enforcing laws concerning wildlife. When two whooping cranes were tragically shot to death in December 2000, it was wildlife officers from the commission who investigated. They were assisted in part by calls on the Wildlife Alert Line.

Wildlife Alert is a new service. Calls made to 1-800-404-FWCC are automatically forwarded to the office nearest the caller. Wildlife officers take reports and forward them to the proper individual for investigation. This phone forwarding system is new, so some agency employees at times may not be aware of the procedure. In cases of confusion, an alternative is to call the main commission number in the Appendix.

Rewards are offered for information about wildlife violations. The rewards are made through the Wildlife Alert Reward Association, a group appointed by the agency's director, that decides what rewards are appropriate. Citizens can accept or decline rewards. There are also provisions which allow the person making the report to remain anonymous.

Wiregrass underlies most of the forest.

In the older longleaf trees, endangered red-cockaded woodpeckers make rare appearances. Occasionally they can be seen flitting from tree to tree, but they are most likely seen by observing an active nest cavity. Active cavities can be located by observing the resin oozing from pitch wells pecked into the tree trunks around the nest holes.

For those who want to see mammals, this forest has much to offer. Beavers make dams in some streams. Otters swim in its waters. White-tailed deer are plentiful among the pines, their namesake white tails raised as they bolt away. Black bear and bobcat, as elsewhere, are elusive.

Amateur or professional botanists can enjoy themselves in many ways. In bogs, pitcher plants can be prolific, including not only the common yellow trumpets, but also the white tops. Many species of vines and wildflowers color the forest.

Equestrian rides and facilities are quite extraordinary. There are stables for 72 horses (and 124 dogs) within the Coldwater Recreation Area. It is possible to ride along scenic Coldwater Creek as well as a number of criss-crossing loops in the Coldwater Recreation Area, which allow the rider to choose from routes of a few miles in length to others many miles long.

Forest Location. The forest is located on the Florida-Alabama border, extending south in places to US-90. The main road through the forest is SR-4, north of (and more or less parallel to) US-90. The forest headquarters is located near the intersection of CR-191 and SR-4 in Munson. Maps are available there showing all trail locations.

Bicycling: Bear Lake Loop, 7 miles (in progress), 1200 miles of forest roads.
Equestrian: Coldwater Creek, 14 miles.
Hiking: Bear Lake Loop, 4 miles; Jackson Trail, 21 miles; Wiregrass Trail, 6 miles.

Managed by: Division of Forestry

BIG LAGOON STATE RECREATION AREA
(Escambia County, 698 acres, bicycling, hiking)

This recreation area offers camping and three trails: a 1.5-mile Flatwoods Pine Trail, The Yaupon Nature Trail of .75 miles, and a 3.5-mile mountain bike trail, called the Cookie Cutter Trail because it was made by a girl scout troop. Bicycles are allowed on the 2.5 miles of paved road, there is some fine sand beach for walking, and there are boardwalks and an observation tower. A good portion of the recreation area is scrub with sand pine. Judging by the paw prints, the area is rich in foxes.

The recreation area is management for Tarkiln Bayou State Preserve, 4 miles north of Big Lagoon on SR-293. The preserve has unmarked service roads and trails, and is home to several species of pitcher plants.

Perdido Key State Recreation Area is also managed by Big Lagoon, and both are on SR-292. Perdido is a barrier island with 2.5 miles of beach.

Big Lagoon is in the extreme west of Florida, to the southwest of Pensacola. Take SR-292 west from Pensacola, and signs will announce the south (left) turn to the site.

BLACKWATER HERITAGE STATE TRAIL
(see Blackwater River State Park)

BLACKWATER RIVER STATE FOREST
(Okaloosa and Santa Rosa counties, 190,000+ acres, multi-use)

For best use of this large and exceptional forest, obtain maps in advance, or at the forest headquarters just south of SR-4 on CR-191 in Munson.

This is not only Florida's largest state forest, but a place of premier hikes, 1200 miles of forest roads (for both bicycling and hiking), and equestrian trails along Coldwater Creek. Both Blackwater River and Coldwater Creek are favorites for canoe trips.

Blackwater draws fishermen to three popular lakes (Bear, Hurricane, and Karrick) engineered in the 1950s. During hunting season, it also draws hunters, and especially on weekends hikers and bicyclists should use caution, or perhaps stay away.

Longleaf pine is the predominant tree, and sandhill is the predominate community. In spring, the ivory blooms of dogwood stand out in the forest, and solitary southern magnolias blossom beneath a sea of towering pines.

BLACKWATER RIVER STATE PARK/ BLACKWATER HERITAGE STATE TRAIL

(Santa Rosa County, multi-use)

Formerly, this small park was best known for the last 2 miles of the Blackwater River Canoe Trail, one of Florida's designated canoe trails, and its two short nature walks. However, it is now the trailhead of the Blackwater Heritage State Trail, mostly a railroad bed converted to paved trail (a "rail-to-trail") for bicyclists and foot traffic. There is a side trail for horse riding, but as of publication, it is not ready for use. The trail currently runs 8.5 miles from Whiting Field Naval Air Station through the town of Milton. A new 1.5-mile section south of US-90 will begin construction in 2003. Bicyclists are required to wear a helmet when riding on federal properties. There are plans to greatly expand this rail-to-trail so that in time it will become a 100-mile circular trail. When completed, it will pass through the Blackwater River State Forest.

This park is reached by turning north off US-90 in the small town of Harold, 7 miles east of Milton.

Top, right: a boardwalk on a trail through Blackwater River State Forest.

Below: a boardwalk through Blackwater River State Park.

Opposite page, top left: equestrian trails pass beside Coldwater Creek in the Coldwater Recreation Area of Blackwater River State Forest.

Opposite page, below left: Coldwater Creek, a popular canoe journey.

Opposite page, top right: a hiker beside a very large southern magnolia, an understory tree in this longleaf pine forest.

(TOM) BROWN PARK
(Leon County, bicycling and hiking).

Located just off busy Capitol Circle in Tallahassee, these trails are a surprising reprieve from honking horns and frazzled motorists. Primarily for Motor Cross quality bicycling, the trails plummet down slopes and wash-outs and cross over logs and jumps for almost 7 miles. The trails are well-marked, but there are many pleasantly distracting, tantalizing side trails. Although blessed with tall trees and large birds of prey, this is not a large natural area, but a super bicycle trail.

From I-10, take the first US-90 exit in Tallahassee when traveling east to west, or the last US-90 exit when travel west to east. Go west toward the city and turn south (or left) on Capitol Circle. A prominent sign announces the left (or east) turn onto the road to the county animal shelter, recreational complex, and the park. In less than a half mile, you are in a quiet woods.

Managed by: City of Tallahassee.

CHIPOLA SEGMENT, FLORIDA TRAIL
(Calhoun and Liberty counties, hiking)

This 28-mile segment of the Florida Trail is currently in transition and lies mostly along roadways, including SR-20. It adjoins the Econfina Creek Segment at Shelton's Corner, then proceeds east over the big bridge at the Apalachicola River at Blounstown, then into the Apalachicola National Forest. Checking with the Florida Trail Association may be a good idea because of anticipated changes. *Managed by: Florida Trail Association.*

CHOCTAWHATCHEE SEGMENT, FLORIDA TRAIL
(Walton and Washington counties, hiking)

The 17-mile Choctawhatchee segment of the Florida Trail is mostly along the SR-20 right-of-way, and runs from Freeport to Ebro. This segment may also be changed in the near future. *Managed by: Florida Trail Association.*

ECONFINA CREEK SEGMENT, FLORIDA TRAIL
(Bay and Washington counties, hiking)

Several Econfinas exist in Florida, including the Econfina River. The word may have meant "earth bridge" in the language of the Native American Creeks. Until recently this 16-mile segment of the Florida Trail ran largely along road rights-of-way. As of 2000, there is an off-road section beginning at SR-20, about 4.4 miles east of CR-77, and running to US-231 near CR-167. *Managed by: Florida Trail Association.*

ECONFINA RIVER SEGMENT, FLORIDA TRAIL
(Madison and Taylor counties, hiking)

The Econfina River flows into the Gulf of Mexico not far from the mouth of the Aucilla River. The Aucilla and Econfina segments of the Florida Trail connect in the Aucilla Wildlife Management Area. The Econfina River Segment passes for 26-miles through pine plantation of the Foley Land and Timber Company. The west end is at the Aucilla River Bridge (west of Perry on US-98). In an understatement, the Florida Trail Association Map (highly recommended for this area) states "only a minor canopy of shade covers most of the route." Before naturalists decide they would rather avoid a pine plantation, it should be noted that bobcats and otters were seen on this trail on several occasions, rare and elusive sights.

ECONFINA RIVER STATE PARK
(Taylor County, 3,400 acres, multi-use)

The Econfina is a 43-mile, blackwater river that flows from swamps in Taylor and Madison counties into the Gulf of Mexico. It is mostly in natural condition, narrow and twisty.

There are 9 miles of multi-use trail. They start from a point near the boat ramp and emerge on CR-14. This is an attractive park with flatwoods, floodplain, hammock, saltmarsh, and a small amount of scrub dominated by sand pine. The trail is marked with a horseshoe sign. There are many deer in this area.

To the west of Perry on US-98, a prominent sign directs the driver south onto CR-14. The road dead-ends at the boat launch. There is a separate area for horse trailer parking.

EGLIN AIR FORCE BASE
(Okaloosa, Santa Rosa, and Walton counties, 460,000+ acres, multi-use)

Although the Eglin portions of the Florida Trail are listed at over 100 miles, these are largely road rights-of-way. Plans are underway, however, to place 50 miles of the trail in the woods. There are also base and range roads, providing access to perhaps the most scenic sections of Eglin. For a map of the base and to avoid interfering with base operations and training, visitors are required to stop at the Natural Resources Office before proceeding.

Since Eglin roads are paved or clay, they can also be biked. When biking on any military installation, the use of a helmet is mandatory.

The Timberlake Trail is a very popular, 6-mile bicycle ride from the Timberlake Campgrounds (Base Road 234 and SR-189). Eglin allows equestrian use.

Enormous Eglin provides the naturalist many surprises. Not the least are its steepheads. The lay of the land seems flat in every direction, but then suddenly you find yourself on the edge of a precipice, looking down on the tops of trees, into a deep canyon filled with lush vegetation. Vast areas of Eglin are longleaf pine woods, while others are sand pine. In some areas, lichen or "deer moss" appear as vast mats.

Eglin is bordered on the north by I-10, and to the south in parts by SR-20 and US-98. Three state roads pass from north to south: SR-85, SR-87, and SR-285. For required recreational permits, first stop at the Natural Resource Office at the Jackson Guard in Niceville. It is on SR-85 south of I-10 or north from SR-20. An annual permit at a modest fee is required.

WILDER-PHOBIA

"An unreasonable fear of the wilderness and the great outdoors."

Some people are uncomfortable when alone in the wilds. When one lonely area was visited by two companions, the first felt overjoyed to be in a remote, isolated area with abundant wildlife. The second was afraid, saying it looked like the type of place someone might bury a body.

One Florida scientist termed this "wilder-phobia," an unreasonable fear, like fear of flying. These fears are very similar. True, once in a while there is plane crash, but the odds of being aboard such a flight are in the millions. Likewise, statistically one is much safer in the wilderness than in one's car or home.

This same scientist suggested that movies might be responsible. In countless films, small groups in the wilderness are killed by maniacs.

Oppposite page, top: black titi in bloom at Eglin Air Force Base.

Opposite page, center: golden club growing in a creek on Eglin Air Force Base. It is found in bogs and streams mainly in North and Northwest Florida.

Left: couple hiking the trail in Florida Caverns State Park.

Below: worn limestone, ferns, oaks, and palms in the gorgeous Chipola River floodplain.

FLORIDA CAVERNS STATE PARK
(Jackson County, 1,280 acres, multi-use)

As surprising as it may seem, Florida has impressive caves, particularly in the northern regions. Florida Caverns is the only one available for public tours.

Outside the caves, four trails (the River, Sink, Service, and Management trails) combine for 3 miles of hiking, while the multi-use Upper Chipola River Recreational Trail is 1.05 miles in and 1.05 miles back, with .70 miles of two off-shooting trails. There are equestrian facilities and overnight camping.

While the caverns are certainly an attraction, the Chipola floodplain and river offer more subtle pleasure. There is a great variety of vegetation and intense natural beauty. The Chipola River flows from Alabama, traveling 80 miles before merging with the Apalachicola.

There are a number of rare creatures found in the park. Barbour's map turtles and alligator snapping turtles are in the river, and the caverns host three species of bats: the eastern pipistrelle, southeastern, and endangered gray bat. The pipistrelle is one of the world's smallest mammals at one-half ounce. The chances are very slim of seeing more than a solitary bat or two in the caves.

Located on SR-167, 3 miles north of Mariana. Prominently marked by signs from I-10 and US-90.

PC

Above: the Florida River as seen from the Florida River Island Trail on a foggy, cold winter morning.

Below, left: a boardwalk on the nature trail at Florida River Island.

PC

FLORIDA RIVER ISLAND TRAIL
(Liberty County, 5,000 acres, bicycling and hiking)

This quiet, isolated island is located in the Florida River on the west side of the Apalachicola National Forest. Outside of hunting season, the visitor can enjoy a private island and experience a separate peace with nature.

Surrounding the island is floodplain with dense forest and plentiful deer. Approximately 10 miles of roads wind around, sometimes impassable with deep, rain-filled potholes, but otherwise easily biked or hiked. Off road, there are two nature trails of 2 and 2.5 miles, and because of creaky, narrow boardwalks, these are suitable only for foot traffic.

Parking is at the end of FR-188 where a sturdy wooden bridge connects the island to the mainland. From Bristol, go south on SR-12, and west on CR-379 to FR-188. *Managed by: Northwest Florida Water Management District.*

GRAYTON BEACH STATE RECREATION AREA
(Walton County, 1,130 acres, hiking)

This recreation area is located between the Gulf of Mexico and brackish Western Lake to the north. It has some of the finest remaining natural beach in Florida. Grayton is a work of restless nature, created by constantly varying waves and winds.

The beach walk is 1 mile each way, and combined with the nature trail, 3 miles of hiking can be achieved. The nature trail has two loops along back dunes, by pine flatwoods, and through coastal scrub.

Grayton lies between Panama City and Ft. Walton Beach. From US-98/30, go south on CR-30A, 1 mile west of Seaside.

GULF ISLANDS NATIONAL SEASHORE
(Escambia, Okaloosa, and Santa Rosa counties, 65,225 acres, including submerged lands, hiking)

This national seashore occupies barrier islands extending west into Alabama. The Florida sections are: Fort Pickens, Perdido Key, Fort Barrancas, the Advanced Redoubt on Pensacola Naval Air Station, Naval Live Oaks, Santa Rosa, and Okaloosa.

There are excellent nature trails and many miles for beach walks. The 22.6-mile Seashore Segment of the Florida Trail begins with an almost 7-mile section at the western end of the Fort Pickens parking lot. From there, an 8.3-mile beach walk connects to the Santa Rosa area.

Located directly south of Pensacola. The major intersecting east-west highway is US-98. Take US-98 to the visitor center at the Naval Live Oaks Area.

Left: a small stream beside the trail in Lake Talquin State Forest.

Above: a paved path through Maclay Gardens.

LAKE TALQUIN STATE FOREST
(Gadsden and Leon counties, 16,326 acres, multi-use)

This forest comprises ten separate tracts. The two along the Ochlockonee River, west of Tallahassee, are the North and South Ochlocknee tracts. There are eight on Lake Talquin's shores: Bear Creek, Bloxham, Fort Braden, Joe Budd, Lines, Midway, Rocky Comfort, and Talquin.

Probably the best trails are within the Fort Braden Tract, where there are 12 miles for equestrian use, and 13-blazed hiking miles maintained by volunteers. The hiking trail can be shortened by taking the Bear Creek or Ravines loops. Bicycling is permitted on open roads, but not footpaths, equestrian trails, or in the Bear Creek Tract.

Within this state forest, inviting trails cross ravines, passing through sandhill, and along the scenic banks of Lake Talquin, a man-made lake. This is a hilly, wooded area, with no flatwoods and little pine, so it is more northern in appearance than most of Florida.

The Fort Braden trailhead is to the west of Tallahassee on SR-20, 5.5 miles west of CR-1585. To navigate between the ten different tracts, a forest map should be requested from the *Division of Forestry.*

MACLAY GARDENS STATE PARK
(Leon County, 1,100 acres, multi-use)

If you are tired of trying to identify plants from photographs the size of postage stamps in various guides, go to Maclay Gardens. If you do not care if it is flea bane or hibiscus, go anyway just for the sight of so many living things. Hundreds of species, including both native and exotic plants, are growing in this awesome garden located on the banks of Lake Hall. When spring comes, the blooms are gorgeous.

Maclay has five trails. The 3.5-mile Lake Trail and the 1.5-mile Ravine Trail are multi-use and located on the Lake Overstreet Tract. The trails are linked by a 0.5-mile connector. In addition, the tract features a 2.8-mile bicycle trail. The Hall Nature Trail and the Boy Scout Trail are located adjacent to Lake Hall Recreation Area. Each of those trails is aproximately 1 mile. Bicycling is also allowed on 1.5 miles of paved roads. Exit I-10 in Tallahassee onto Thomasville Road (US-319), a very busy thoroughfare. The entrance to the Gardens is a short distance north on the west side of the road, and easy to miss in the heavy traffic.

OCHLOCKONEE RIVER STATE PARK
(Wakulla County, 392 acres, bicycling and hiking).

The combined length of the Flatwoods and River hiking trails aproaches 2 miles. There is a car trail, open to bicycling and hiking, of 1.4 miles with benches where red-cockaded woodpeckers are often observed. The paved road can also be bicycled. There are service roads open to hiking, and camping options.

The park is the management unit for 1,300-acre Bald Point. This is near where the Ochlockonee joins the Gulf, and has 3 miles of shore. Otherwise, there are presently no trails.

The state park is 4 miles south of Sopchoppy on US-319. For Bald Point, turn south from US-98 on SR-370, then east on Bald Point Road.

POINT WASHINGTON STATE FOREST
(Walton County, 15,170 acres, bicycling and hiking)

The Eastern Lake Trail is a long loop of 10 miles, shortened by cross trails to either 3.5 or 5 miles. Bicycling and hiking are allowed, but bicyclists should note it's sandy out there. Camping is allowed with permit. Unlike most forests, there is no equestrian use.

As can be expected of such a large area, it has a variety of habitats including flatwoods, lake, marsh, ponds, sandhill, scrub, and swamps. Coyotes are sometimes seen beneath the longleaf and sandpine (actually they are a fairly common sight along many Panhandle roads).

From US-98, south on CR-395. The forest is roughly equidistant from Panama City and Ft. Walton Beach. CR-30A to the south is along the beach. Grayton Beach State Recreation Area is to the west, and a combined visit can more than fill a day.

Managed by: Division of Forestry.

(ELINOR KLAPP) PHIPPS PARK
(Leon County, 9,000 acres, multi-use)

This park is located to the northeast of Lake Jackson. When last visited, the portion at the lake was closed. The conditions on the banks of Jackson can change quickly. The lake is frequently drained through sinkholes during drought and periods of low rainfall, but can fill to overflowing during heavy rains.

The bicycle trail is referred to as the Red Bug Trail. Red bugs are also known as chiggers, pesky mite-like creatures capable of inflicting an itching bite. The Florida Trail loop is 6.7 miles, but much more distance is available using a combination of side trails. Equestrian use is allowed with city permit.

Located north of Tallahassee, along CR-155 to the east of Lake Jackson.

Managed by: City of Tallahassee.

Above, left: **a lovely canopy road near Phipps Park in Tallahassee.**

Above, right: **a view of Eastern Lake in Point Washington State Forest.**

PINE LOG STATE FOREST
(Bay and Washington counties, 6,911 acres, multi-use)

Pine Log has the distinction of being Florida's first state forest (1936) and is named for a tannin-colored creek. It is quiet, isolated, usually lightly used, and a great place to spot bluebirds.

The 9-mile round trip Crooked Creek Trail, is a multi-use trail developed primarily for mountain bikes. Eight miles of the Florida Trail pass through Pine Log. Shorter trails are the Campground Trail at 2 miles and Dutch Tieman at 4 miles, both part of the Trailwalker Program of the Division of Forestry. Many bicyclists recommend the Tieman Trail. Camping is allowed with permit. A forest map is very helpful and can be obtained from the Division of Forestry.

Habitats: flatwoods, forest, lakes, marsh, ponds, river, sandhill, and swamp.

Pine Log is located off SR-79, 4 miles south of Ebro.

Managed by: Division of Forestry.

ONE TERRIFIC VALUE
Most Florida parks and recreation areas charge a small fee. This money helps to maintain them and keep them open. An annual individual or family pass to Florida's parks is an outstanding value. Less than the cost of a one-day ticket to most of Florida's theme parks, an annual park pass entitles the user to enjoy an exceptional variety of beautiful and wondrous places: beaches, caverns, forests, gardens, lakes, rivers, and thousands of miles of trail in natural settings. Only a few visits will result in a substantial savings over paying one-time entrance fees.

SO FAR FROM HOME

The wildlife at St. George is usually predictable: beach mice and raccoons in the dunes, ghost crabs and birds along the seashore. In 1999, this park received a visitor incredibly out of place, a snowy owl.

In the preface to Ernest Hemingway's famous short story, **The Snows of Kilimanjaro,** *the carcass of a leopard was found on the slopes of that African mountain. There was great speculation what he had been seeking at such a height. This snowy owl was much more out of place.*

Snowy owls are Arctic birds, which normally do not come any closer to Florida than the beaches of New York or New Jersey. The St. George snow bird was at least 1,000 miles out of its normal range

Its presence so far south in the fall of 1999 attracted hundreds of birders. Maybe the owl was disoriented, driven by a scarcity of prey, or just traveling on whimsy. But once at St. George, the owl probably dined on mice living in the dunes.

(FRED GANNON) ROCKY BAYOU STATE RECREATION AREA

(Okaloosa County, 357 acres, bicycling and hiking).

Bicycling is allowed on the paved roads, and hiking takes place on three trails totaling 4 miles: Red Cedar, Rocky Bayou, and Sand Pine. The first two are shorter, and Sand Pine is about 2 miles. The area is primarily scrub dominated by sand pine, with lichen prolific on the ground, among various scrub flowers. From I-10, east of Crestview, take SR-285 south toward Fort Walton Beach. Turn east (left) on SR-20 and proceed to the recreation area on the north side of the road.

ST. ANDREWS STATE RECREATION AREA

(Bay County, 1,260 acres, bicycling and hiking).

Many locations in Florida, includng most of those named for saints, were given their names by Florida's early Spanish adventurers. St. Andrews is at the easternmost tip of the peninsula directly southwest of Panama City across St. Andrews Bay. There are two hiking trails of 1.25 miles, and 1.5 miles of gorgeous beach.

The recreation area is management for Shell Island, a barrier island to the east of the recreation area. A shuttle service carries visitors to the narrow (one-quarter mile), but long (7 miles) island, where there is perhaps 1 mile of

Above: **dunes and flowers along the trail at St. George Island State Park.**

hiking, including a boardwalk.

After crossing the Hathaway Bridge heading west from Panama City on US-98, turn south on CR-3031 and follow it to the recreation area.

ST. GEORGE ISLAND STATE PARK

(Franklin County, 1,900 acres, bicycling and hiking)

The eastern end of the island is in the state park, including 9 miles of pristine beach with dunes. Barrier islands, like St. George, take the brunt of hurricanes, offering some degree of protection to the mainland. A 2-mile trail passes through the scrub and skirts a bit of marsh. Raccoons scampering over the dunes make an enjoyable sight around sunrise or sunset. These are terrific beaches for walking. One can take in the sound of the surf, and the face of the Gulf. Bicycles can be ridden on the paved road.

St. George Island is located quite close to a number of other destinations featured in this book. A visit to St. George could easily be combined with visits to Apalachicola River Wildlife and Environmental Area, Tate's Hell State Forest, or St. Vincents National Wildlife Refuge.

From Eastpoint on US-98, follow the signs to the bridge connecting the island to the mainland.

ST. JOSEPH PENINSULA STATE PARK
(Gulf County, 2,515 acres, bicycling and hiking)

Once a barrier island, St. Joseph is now connected by a bayhead to the mainland. The Gulf side of the peninsula has tall, towering, white sand dunes, while the bay side has smaller, rolling dunes dotted with scrub vegetation and sand pine.

The Gulf dunes evoke the expression: "must be seen to be believed." Some have been reported to be as much as 200 feet high. Dunes are dynamic, constantly changing, building up or down, or shifting with the winds.

This is a premier beach walk, but there are also substantial trails. In addition to shorter nature walks, a hiking trail along the bay is 9-miles long, but the hiker has to decide whether to proceed onto the beach to return, or turn around and walk 9 miles back. Also, there are

numerous small, beckoning paths leading from the bay trail, creating diversions and opportunities for irresistible side trips.

Bicycles can be ridden on the paved roads, which approach 10 miles in total length. Along these roads are some ponds and marsh where deer sometimes linger. With no hunting on the peninsula, the deer rarely bolt. There are cabins by reservation, and RV camping.

From US-98 to the west of Apalachicola, turn west on CR-30A, and follow the signs.

Top: a portion of the 9-mile hiking trail on the bay side of St. Joseph Peninsula State Park.

Above, left: a path through high sand dunes leading to the pristine beach at St. Joseph Peninsula State Park.

Above, right: sea oats adorning sand dunes in the Panhandle. Sea oats can reach a height of 6 feet. They are actually a kind of coarse grass which grows in clumps. The seeds mature usually in late summer or fall.

ST. MARKS NATIONAL WILDLIFE REFUGE

(Jefferson, Taylor, and Wakulla counties, 100,000 acres, multi-use)

This large refuge has long trails brimming with wildlife: alligators, bears, bobcats, numerous bird species, and plentiful deer.

Stopping at the headquarters for maps is essential to finding one's way around and making the most of a visit. It is also necessary to pay fees either for day use or by an annual pass (the annual pass is the best bargain).

St. Marks includes fresh and saltwater impoundments with levees for access. It also has flatwoods, hammock, marsh, scrub, and swamps.

At present, the refuge is in three segments: the eastern, central, and western. The headquarters is 4 miles south of US-98 from Newport on CR-59. This is west of Perry and south of Tallahassee.

Bicycling: 8 paved miles, 20 on grass dike tops.

Equestrian: allowed on St. Marks. Parking is in front of the visitor's center. Group users on weekends should call in advance.

Hiking Trails, Eastern Segment: Stoney Bayou (6 miles) and Deep Creek (12 miles) are essentially the same trail, with Stoney Bayou a shorter loop. These trails offer birding and wildlife observation, but are not the most scenic trails within the refuge.

Dike trails: (20 miles) pass by freshwater impoundment and saltmarsh. Tree islands or hammocks can be seen in the distance.

Hiking Trails, Central Segment: Visitor's Center, Port Leon Road, 3 miles. Stardust Loop, 5 miles.

Hiking Trails, Western Segment: Blue Springs Loop, 4 miles, is one of the most scenic trails within the refuge and can be accessed off the equally breath-taking, nearby Florida Trail, starting from the Wakulla Beach Road Trailhead to the south of US-98. Purify Bay Loop, 5 miles. Otter Lake Loop, 9 miles, when last visited, was an un-blazed, difficult to follow walk in woods around pristine Otter Lake. Ridge Trail, 5 miles.

Florida Trail: More than 43 miles of the Florida Trail are designated. Maps are also available through the Florida Trail Association.

Top, left: cypress at Otter Lake, a remote and wild area of St. Marks National Wildlife Refuge.

Top, right: a marsh alongside a trail in St. Marks National Wildlife Refuge. Swamps have trees, while marshes have no trees.

Below, left: Gerry Bishop, editor of *Ranger Rick,* the premier children's nature magazine, takes a photo of a thistle along Stoney Bayou Trail.

ST. VINCENT NATIONAL WILDLIFE REFUGE
(Franklin County, 12,360 acres, hiking)

Wild and primitive St. Vincent Island has over 80 miles of hiking trail, with no overnight camping permitted. The trails are on forest roads created when the island was lumbered.

Southwest of the city of Apalachicola, and a stone's throw from land, the bay side of this barrier island is saltmarsh with alligators. The Gulf beach is dense with palms and rolling dunes. It doesn't get any wilder than this in Florida.

Exotic wildlife was imported when St. Vincent was a private hunting preserve. These included zebra, but most exotics are gone now. Two remaining are feral hogs and the Asian sambar deer, a large species of elk, reaching up to 700 pounds. Sambar can be spotted drinking at one of the freshwater lakes on the island. St. Vincent now also has red wolves introduced by the US Fish and Wildlife Service.

The interior trails of St. Vincent are rugged walks through sand, and there are no water fountains nor toilets. All supplies must be brought in by backpack. Summer high temperatures have felled at least one visitor. There are also biting insects and venomous snakes on the island, and while the most likely problem is discomfort, this is not a theme park,

or a trip for the faint of heart.

Visitors should first stop at the Visitor Center in Apalachicola. Access to the island is possible only by boat. It is a short trip, but if there is stormy weather, it can be a treacherous ride from Indian Pass, west of Apalachicola. Guides are available to taxi visitors to the island. Guide referrals are available from the Chamber of Commerce on US-98 in downtown Apalachicola. From there, it is a short drive following the signs to the refuge headquarters.

TALLAHASSEE-ST. MARKS TRAIL
(Leon and Wakulla counties, multi-use)

The state's first "rail-to-trail" is mostly suburban. It is 19 miles of paved path from a trailhead by a busy Tallahassee highway to the comparatively sleepy town of St. Marks. Historic Fort San Marcos and St. Marks National Wildlife Refuge are nearby. There is a parallel equestrian trail. The 7.5-mile Munson Hill Off-Road Trail is a loop that departs into longleaf pine flatwoods and sandhill of the Apalachicola National Forest. When the railroad opened in 1837, this track was hacked through untamed wilderness and must have been a major undertaking. Northern terminus: just south of Capital Circle (SR-261) on SR-363 in Tallahassee. Southern terminus: three blocks from the dead-end of SR-363 at the St. Marks River.

Above: **the wild and primitive bayside of St. Vincent National Wildlife Refuge.**

THREE RIVERS STATE RECREATION AREA
(Jackson County, 682 acres, bicycling and hiking).

On rolling hills beside Lake Seminole are two hiking trails of approximately 2.75 miles, and 2 miles of shoreline. The shorter trail, Half-Dry Creek, is aptly named, and a little hard to follow. It is located next to the parking area. By the campground, the longer Lakeside Trail can be found. Bicycling is allowed on the paved roads. From I-10, go north on SR-286 to Sneads, turn west on US-90, then north on SR-271. There are prominent signs.

FLORIDA'S MYSTERY CAT

The jaguarundi with its long tail looks superficially otter-like, but runs like a cat. It is normally found in the Southwest and Central America. Rangers at St. Marks report several jaguarundi sightings and believe this animal has become established here. However, some scientists are skeptical. One argument against the presence of jaguarundi is the lack of road kills. On the other hand, portions of St. Marks are lonely, isolated, and mostly far from the highway.

TATE'S HELL STATE FOREST
(Liberty and Franklin counties, 144,508 acres, multi-use)

At present, the forest is mostly accessed from multi-use roads. The roads vary greatly, from hard and firm, to sandy and squishy. There is also a 1-mile High Bluff Coastal Nature Trail located 4 miles west of Carrabelle on US-98. There are plans are to add additional segments annually.

Many have asked about Tate's Hell. It is a new, large area, attracting much curiosity. Undoubtedly, in time this large forest will offer many pleasurable recreational opportunities. However, the main impression is that it needs time to recover from substantial lumbering by private timber companies before it will be an enjoyable place. The lumbering preceded the state acquisition.

The colorful name is from a local settler, who, according to legend, pursued into the swamp a wildcat that had killed his livestock. Lost for several days, Tate abandoned his shotgun, lost his dogs, never found the wildcat, and was bitten by a water moccasin. When found by locals, and asked where he had been, he said he had been to Hell.

Tate's Hell is directly south of Apalachicola National Forest, perhaps a half hour east of the city of Apalachicola on US-98, between SR-65 and US-319. It can best be accessed from the east side of SR-65. Contact Tate's Hell Forest from the information in the Appendix prior to a visit for the most up-to-date information.

Managed by: Division of Forestry.

Right: blooming sawgrass along Cashie Bayou, Tate's Hell State Forest.

Below: the dunes, beach, and waters of Topsail Hill Reserve all remain in a natural state.

TOPSAIL STATE PRESERVE/GREGORY E. MOORE RV RESORT
(Walton County, 18,000 acres, hiking)

This preserve has as much as 5 miles of hiking, depending on how one goes about it. Major habitats: beach, coastal forest, dunes, and lakes, including freshwater lakes. The beach is splendid and untouched, a reprieve from heavily populated, congested Destin. The preserve is 13 miles east of Destin on US-98.

Managed by: Grayton Beach State Recreation Area.

THE NOVICE BICYCLIST

Bikes with narrow tires, made for speed, can be used on paved trails like the Tallahassee-St. Marks. Any bike will suffice on a paved path. But off-road riding, over roots and through sand, requires a different kind of bicycle. There are combination bicycles, or hybrids, claiming to perform well on both surfaces, but a wide-tire, multi-gear bicycle, called a "mountain" bike is what is usually recommended for off-road conditions.

The novice should not let the name "mountain" bike intimidate. It is not a large bike, nor do you have to ride over mountains, or have the strength necessary to do so. It will be slower and a little harder going on paved paths than a regular bike, and for that reason many bicyclists end up owning both wide and narrow-tire bikes.

For those who have never tried it, off-road riding is at first a little scary because of the potential falls. If you ride a bicycle long enough, no matter how talented, you will fall sooner or later. Thus, the first accessory necessary for a would-be bicyclist, whether off or on-road, is not a rear view mirror, or a cup holder, but a helmet.

And it's true–once you know how to ride a bycicle, you never forget!

Left: a road in Torreya State Park in autumn.

Above: a tree fallen across a ravine in Torreya.

TORREYA STATE PARK
(Liberty County, 2,500 acres, bicycling and hiking)

Botanists speak of Torreya State Park with a twinkle in their eye, as if they are sharing a wonderful secret. They are. Torreya is a jewel in the state park system.

In the last ice age, this area sheltered plants and trees which could not survive in colder, more northern areas. Descendants of some of these ice age fugitives can still be found at Torreya. Called relict species, they include the tree that is the park's namesake–the torreya tree. Another tree with dwindling numbers is the Florida yew, found in some isolated spots. A long list of plant and tree species is available from the ranger's office, including perhaps 120 thought to be rare, threatened, or endangered.

From the bluff behind Gregory House, there are stunning views of the Apalachicola River. The changing of the leaves adds fall color to the beauty. The trails, often up and down slopes and ravines, can be difficult, especially when wet. There is even a small waterfall on the Weeping Ridge Trail.

Major habitats: floodplain, ravines, river, sandhill, and streams. The woods here are considered either slope forest or uplands. Torreya offers a variety of camping, including a yurt tent.

Bicycle trail: 3 miles.

Hiking: Rock Creek Trail, 7 miles. Stone Bridge Trail, 1 mile. Torreya Trail, 7 miles. Weeping Ridge Trail, 3 miles.

Located south of I-10, west of Tallahassee. Between Bristol and Greensboro, exit SR-12 onto CR-1641, and follow the signs.

UNIVERSITY OF WEST FLORIDA
(Escambia County, bicycling and hiking).

This is a beautiful campus north of Pensacola. There is a 4-mile trail leading from the jogging course and a much longer course leading from the tower directly across from Campus Information. While the procedure is to check in with Campus Information to obtain a parking permit, don't expect them to know anything about the trails. The trails are up and down, through forests and sandhill. The bicycling is difficult with many possible jumps for the daring.

Traveling west on I-10, take the first exit north immediately after the bridge across Escambia Bay, or if traveling east, the last exit before the bay. This is US-90, a scenic route. At the junction with Alternate US-90, turn west (or left). The first two roads to the north lead onto the campus.

WAKULLA SPRINGS STATE PARK
(Wakulla County, 4,700 acres, multi-use)

Sometimes an incredible one billion gallons of water flows from Wakulla in just one day. This is one of the deepest, largest, and most powerful springs in the world, and it contains what may be the biggest underwater cave system. If you dine in Wakulla Lodge, you will be sitting over an enormous cavern large enough to contain a sixteen-story building.

More than 300 Florida springs are powerful enough to be named. Those with the greatest water output are called first-magnitude springs. There are 27, including Wakulla, but perhaps it should be in a class of its own.

Tour boats travel down river, and glass-bottom boats drift over the crystal clear spring. The Wakulla River outside the park is one of the prime canoe and kayak journeys in Florida.

While the springs and river are the main reason to visit, this is gorgeous land with a 2.5-mile nature trail. There is a 7-mile, multi-use trail. The equestrian area has ample parking.

Located south of Tallahassee 16 miles, and 4 miles west of Wakulla, on SR-267 at SR-61.

SHORTER NORTHWEST TRAILS

PONCE DE LEON SPRINGS STATE RECREATION AREA
(Washington County)

Two short trails pass by the spring and along creeks. The floodplain is mostly hardwood swamp. Located off I-10, north of the town of Ponce de Leon, clearly marked by signs.

PITT SPRING
(Washington County)

Part of the Econfina Creek Water Management Area, Pitt Spring has almost 3 miles of hiking trail winding along the creek. The creek also provides an exceptional canoe journey, perhaps the most strenuous in Florida. Located on the north side of SR-20, north of Panama City about 30 miles.

RIVER BLUFF STATE PICNIC SITE
(Leon County)

Two miles of trail in two loops pass up and down steep ravines and over a boardwalk at Lake Talquin. Combine this one with the Lake Talquin State Forest. Located ten miles west of Tallahassee on SR-20 at Jack Vause Road.

Above: Ponce de Leon Spring runs 350 feet before flowing into Sandy Creek, a tributary of the Choctawhatchee river. Spring Run Trail is along a portion of the run.

Left: an osprey with captured prey, a mullet.

PLEASURABLE SHORT TRAILS

Many people begin their outdoor adventures on short trails. The three areas mentioned on this page are examples of why short trails might be good places to start exploring. All three are very scenic. None are overly long, difficult, or taxing. Short trails are great places to initiate children to the joys of nature and recreation in the great outdoors, because children might lose interest or become discouraged on longer, more difficult trips.

North Florida has the two longest rivers in the state, the St. Johns (273 miles) and the Suwannee (originating in Georgia with 177 miles within Florida). These rivers, their tributaries, and springs do much to define the adjacent areas.

The region has many small places of interest and it is possible to combine them for weekend or longer trips with many of the excellent state parks, preserves, and recreation areas. Within the Suwannee River Water Management District alone, there are over 20 district lands, mostly multi-use. The St. Johns district has 40 sites offering recreation, multi-use in most cases, stretching a considerable distance from the area north of Jacksonville to the St. Johns River headwaters in Central Florida.

Two large national forests, the Osceola and Ocala, provide many opportunities for memorable explorations. The Ocala is a favorite of many, in part because of its spring runs. The Osceola is the wildest national forest in the state. This is particularly true of its northern lands which border the Okefenokee Swamp in Georgia, the headwaters of the Suwannee River.

There are many remote areas within this region with no ranger safety net. On these lands, adventurers are more or less on their own. In areas around the Alapaha River or the northern Suwannee, for example, it is a good idea to travel in twos or threes, with well stocked backpacks and a compass. Hikers in particular should not reach for more than they are capable, and should try to accurately judge their stamina and endurance.

Before worrying unduly about entering wild, remote Florida, consider how much safer and easier it is than, say, the public lands of the western US. Florida is flat, and there are no deserts without water. Probably most people would not want to chance drinking the water on Florida's wilderness lands, but in an emergency, it could be done. Upon becoming lost, it would usually be possible to find a nearby river and follow it, sooner or later arriving at a bridge and a road. In the wilds of the American West, the river might be interrupted by a gorge not so easily crossed. Furthermore, there might be cougars and grizzlies which could pose a danger to a hiker. While Florida is safer than many

parts of the US, it is not free of all perils. Preparation and common sense are the best guides to safe enjoyment.

Top: a field of phlox in spring.

Above: a luna moth.

SI-JM

ALLARDT TRACT
(Hamilton County, 188 acres, multi-use)

With a half-mile on the Suwannee River, Allardt is a small jewel in the water management district. It is a little tough to find. From north of Live Oak on US-129, take CR-132 west, then go north on CR-795. The trick to turning north on CR-795 is finding it, as there might not be any sign. From CR-795, without much announcement, 24th Street breaks away on a dirt road to the right. The entrance is suddenly on your left. Drive down a narrow road that appears to be going onto a farm until reaching the trailhead. *Managed by: Suwannee River Water Management District.*

ALLEN MILL POND CONSERVATION AREA
(Lafayette County, 461 acres, bicycling and hiking)

Although some water management districts have locked gates with pedestrian passageways, the Suwannee River district's lands seem to be always open, and cars can be driven in. But one of the reasons you might prefer to park your car and bike or hike into many areas was illustrated when a tree fell, blocking the road in this area.

The road/trails must be retraced out, making this easily over 3 miles. Oaks draped with resurrection fern shade the roads.

Allen Mill Pond is located northwest of Mayo. Go four miles west of Mayo on US-27, then turn north onto CR-251B. Proceed 5 miles on CR-251B to the entrance which is marked with a sign.

Managed by: Suwannee River Water Management District.

AMELIA ISLAND STATE RECREATION AREA
See Talbot GeoPark

Left: water disappearing into underground channels in the Alapaha River.

Below: a pine lily, found in flatwoods and prairies.

SE

ALAPAHA RIVER BASIN CONSERVATION AREA
(Hamilton County, 1750 acres, multi-use)

The acreage mentioned above is for the two most accessible of four conservation areas: the Upper Alapaha and the Jennings Bluff tracts.

There are both trails and dirt roads, in somewhat rugged condition, in the Upper Alapaha Tract and there is a well-maintained road through the Jennings Bluff Tract. The total mileage is not known. There are at least 3 miles in the Jennings Bluff Tract and many more in the Upper Alapaha.

These tracts are so pleasing to the eye that a photograph taken here by naturalist Jeff Ripple graces the cover of the water management district recreation guide.

Sometimes the Alapaha River is extremely low, perhaps two-thirds sand and one third trickling stream. During high-water periods, however, the water can rush through in a fury on its way to join the Suwannee River to the southwest.

For the Upper Alapaha, take CR-143 at the Jennings exit on I-75. After passing through the Jennings' stoplight, make a right on poorly marked CR-150. This road is heading east, although at first it seems that one is going south. The Upper Alapaha tract is easily found after crossing the Alapaha bridge.

The Jennings Bluff Tract is in the midst of farms and homes. Exit from I-75 and drive to Jasper, then proceed north on US-41. Turn east onto Jennings Bluff Road, and follow its twists and turns until reaching the markers for the trailhead.

Managed by: Suwannee River Water Management District.

ANASTASIA STATE PARK
(St. Johns County, 1,200 acres, bicycling and hiking)

Four miles of Atlantic beach, a 1-mile nature trail, and 4 miles of service roads for bicycling and hiking are available for use. There is a large camping area, and a very popular fishing spot. The dunes at Anastasia are wisely protected from destructive human intrusion by a fence. This is a very attractive area, with tall dunes, and a towering lighthouse. Anastasia is thought to be a corruption of Santa Estacia, a name given the island by early Spanish explorers. Located on A1A in St. Augustine Beach, prominently marked by signs.

Right: the gorgeous beach at Anastasia State Park. In the distance, a fence halts dune erosion.
Below: sunrise over Salt Run in Anastasia State Park.
Bottom: a pond in Andrews Wildlife Management Area.

ANDREWS WILDLIFE MANAGEMENT AREA
(Levy County, 3,800 acres, bicycling and hiking)

Like so many areas along the Suwannee River, there is a naturally rich variety of vegetation at Andrews, the largest hardwood forest that borders the Suwannee. Some of the trees here have won recognition for their size, including basswood, birch, elm, and sweetgum. Presently three trees are record holders: a bluff oak, a maple, and a persimmon.

There are many shaded, criss-crossing roads which, when combined, amount to a considerable distance, and most are good for bicycling. No equestrian use is allowed. There are approximately 10 miles of maintained hiking trails. A brochure with a map is available at the kiosk.

This area is 5 miles north of Chiefland. Go west from US-19 at the prominent sign.

Managed by: Florida Fish and Wildlife Conservation Commission.

BAY CREEK CONSERVATION AREA
(Columbia County, 1,904 acres, multi-use)

This is one of three adjoining, true wilderness areas along the banks of the Suwannee River, south of Georgia. This tract is open for multi-use. The others are the Cypress Creek and Benton conservation areas. While they are a joy to any naturalist, these tracts are not for those expecting interpretive signs, or even clear directions. The tracts are mostly floodplain, pine woods, and river. They contain lots of wildlife. From I-75, go east through Jasper on SR-6. After crossing the Suwannee River, the tract is immediately on the south side. *Managed by: Suwannee River Water Management District.*

BAYARD CONSERVATION AREA
(Clay County, 9898 acres, multi-use)

Located on the western banks of the St. Johns, Bayard has interweaving trails in floodplain, hardwood hammock, pine flatwoods, and sandhill, where deer and hawks are frequently seen. Views of the St. Johns River, seen though cypress at the eastward end of the trails, are quite stunning. Depending on how they are traveled, the distance is from 2 or 3 miles to more then 10. Located south of Jacksonville. Bayard is on the south side of SR-16, one-half mile west of the Shands Bridge. *Managed by: St. Johns River Water Management District.*

BEARDSLEY TRACT
(Gilchrist County, 423 acres, hiking)

There are 2 miles of path along the banks of the Suwannee River, north from the landing. Any trail or path along the Suwannee can be considered premier. It is 4 miles round-trip, because at the end of the water management property, you must turn around and hike back. This is not an official trail, nor is it maintained by anyone, other than the animals, hikers, and fishermen making use of it.

Take SR-26 northeast from Fanning Springs. After traveling a short distance, make a sharp left turn onto CR-232. This county road might not be not marked with any sign. Beardsley is at the end of SW 10th Street.

Managed by: Suwannee River Water Management District.

BENTON CONSERVATION AREA
(Columbia County, 750 acres, bicycling and hiking)

Located on the eastern bank of the Suwannee River near Georgia, this is an isolated area suitable only for the self-reliant. There are unblazed trails through substantial areas of floodplain and pine woods. These firm trails are open for hiking and bicycling.

The water management district, fond of the concept of "recreational hubs," could consider this a hub for those who like their outdoors primitive. On the south side of SR-6 is the Bay Creek Tract, and to the north just before the Suwannee is the Cypress Creek Conservation Area. All combine for more than 4,000 acres of quietude amidst wildlife.

From I-75, go east on SR-6 through and beyond Jasper. The Benton Tract is on the north side of the road just after the Suwannee River. There are several parking areas.

Managed by: Suwannee River Water Management District.

Top: Crystal Lake Ravine along the Florida Trail in North Florida.

FLORIDA'S LONGEST RIVER

The St. Johns River is the longest in Florida. This is a north-flowing river, an oddity. Out of Florida's 23 major rivers, only the St. Johns and the St. Marys (which marks the border between Florida and Georgia in the east) flow into the Atlantic. All 273 miles of the St. Johns are within Florida. This river is fed by many springs, including some which are first magnitude. The headwaters of the St. Johns River historically have been in Central Florida marsh systems. The St. Johns is generally much wider than Florida's second longest river, the Suwannee.

FLORIDA'S LONG AND MAGNIFICENT RIVER

Like many Floridians, the Suwannee comes from another state. Its headwaters are in the Okefenokee Swamp in Georgia. As it flows south, water pours in from many springs and tributaries. At times of heaviest flow, the place where these waters meet can be violent and turbulent.

The Suwannee is Florida's second longest river, with 177 miles within the state. The wider, longer St. Johns would probably lose a beauty contest between the two, if it was judged by canoe enthusiasts. This is in part due to the Suwannee's lovely, high banks, scenic bridges, and wooded forests.

BIG SHOALS PUBLIC LANDS
(Hamilton County, 3,510 acres, including former units Big Shoals State Forest, Big Shoals State Park, and Big Shoals Wildlife Management Area, multi-use)

Here is a sight that a visitor will always remember: whitewater in Florida. When the level of water in the river allows, the able visitor should take time to cautiously climb down the short cliff to the banks to listen, to watch, and to be mesmerized by the rushing waters of the Suwannee pouring over the outcrops of limestone. Depending on water level, the Suwannee has other whitewater spots, but these are the most persistent. While some people go over the rapids in canoes and even inner tubes, others portage around the shoals.

The Rapids Trail is approximately a 3-mile trip each way. Mountain bikers sometimes use it, although this is not allowed. A paved bicycle path is planned that will not approach the shoals, but instead, will travel along a forest road. At present, there is also the Long Branch Loop Trail north of the Rapids Trail, also popular with both bicyclists and hikers.

From White Springs, go northeast on CR-135, then turn right on Godwin Bridge Road to the recreational area for the shoals. The main entrance is on CR-135.

Top, left, Top, right, and Opposite page: several views of Big Shoals.
Above: a hiker listens to the rushing water at Steinhatchee Falls, another whitewater river within the Suwannee River Water Management District.

PC

BIG TALBOT ISLAND STATE PARK
See Talbot GeoPark

BLACK CREEK RAVINES CONSERVATION AREA
(Clay County, 965 acres, equestrian and hiking)

On a foggy, spring morning, dewdrops can be heard dripping from the abundant turkey oaks. On bushes and small trees, thousands of filmy-dome spider webs, as well as the webs of a few orb spiders, reflect in the morning sunlight, creating a glorious sight.

The trails back and forth approach a total of 5 miles, and are open for hiking and horse riding. It is too sandy for most bikers, and bicycles are not allowed. To reach Black Creek, an 80-foot overlook, and the ravines, do not follow the urge to turn back at the power line, but continue. You might come across pitcher plants and occasionally spot otters in the creek.

From Starke, go north on US-301 to CR-218. Turn east, and proceed southeast almost to Middleburg. Turn north on Green Road. Go about 1 mile to the trailhead.

Managed by: St. Johns River Water Management District.

BULOW PLANTATION RUINS STATE HISTORIC SITE/BULOW CREEK STATE PARK
(Flagler and Volusia counties, 3,391 acres, bicycling and hiking).

In the early 1800s, the plantation produced sugar, and shipped it to Jacksonville, St. Augustine, and the Caribbean. The sugar was used to produce "demon rum." The Seminoles burned the plantation to the ground during the Second Seminole War, but the ruins remain, mostly covered with green liverwort.

The road into the historic site, as well as the roads inside, are open to bicycling. The Florida Trail Assocation maintains a 4-mile loop for hiking. The trailhead is on the south side of the road into the site. There are also two very short nature trails at the plantation. The plantation loop trail is connected to the state park by a trail of approximately 3 miles. This trail can be hiked or bicycled. There is also a very short nature trail at the park.

The historic site is south of St. Augustine. Exit I-95 at SR-100, and take the first road to the south. This is Old Kings Road, although it appears as CR-2001 on many maps. The state park is announced by prominent signs farther south on Old Kings Road in Volusia County.

BRANFORD RAIL-TO-TRAIL
(Suwannee County)

This paved rail-to-trail is variously described as between 4.7 and 6 miles, running west from Branford. It is probably the shorter distance. Construction has begun on a 7-mile extension to Ichetucknee Springs. The trail currently starts at the junction of SR-129 and US-27, and has also been called the Suwannee River Greenway-Branford. *Managed by: Suwannee River Water Management District.*

BRANTLEY TRACT, LITTLE RIVER CONSERVATION AREA
(Suwannee County, 2,405 acres, multi-use)

The trails in this tract are service roads which encircle and criss-cross the property. There are also 2.6 miles of the Suwannee banks to wander along. About one-third of the area is pine plantation, and another third timbered land. From Branford, go north 7 miles on CR-129, then west on CR-349 for 2 miles, then south for 2 miles on Brantley Road. *Managed by: Suwannee River Water Management District.*

Top: filmy-dome spider webs on a foggy morning at Black Creek Ravine Conservation Area.

Above: a couple walking along the connecting trail from Bulow Creek State Park to the loop at Bulow Plantation Ruins State Historic Site.

CAMP BLANDING
(Clay County, 62,340 acres, multi-use)

While there is but one post, in the minds of visitors it may seem that there are four quite different Camp Blandings. The most northern part is divided by SR-16 into a wildlife management area (usually securely locked and fenced in). A military installation is to the south, complete with security fence and smartly dressed military police.

However, the area off SR-21, to the northwest of Gold Head Branch State Park is usually open to the public for fishing in two lakes, and hiking a portion of the Florida Trail. Horse riding is permitted, and there are miles of roads to bicycle. In between the recreational area, and the active military base, lies an artillery range permanently closed to the public.

For the best use of this section of the Florida Trail, obtain a map from the Florida Trail Association, and plan your start and exit points in advance. Camp Blanding is part of a 24-mile Florida Trail segment running from Starke into Gold Head Branch and ending at the Keystone Airport. It will do no good to show up at the military installation and ask for directions. The mission is training National Guardsmen, not directing hikers, and you will just be sent to nearby Gold Head Branch State Park.

The best procedure is to phone the number in Appendix A for Range Control for permission to cross Camp Blanding. A portion of the trail adjoins a private hunting club and is mostly along the shadeless fence line. There is also an excessively sunny stretch leaving the camp and moving to the trail through Gold Head Branch.

On Camp Blanding, the trail passes along Lowry Lake and beneath towering trees in an area that appears to have never been logged. Along the way, there are scenic ravines, some of the northernmost interior scrub in Florida, and sandhill. Smaller, but equally scenic, Magnolia Lake is near the south entrance to Blanding. The Florida Trail crosses the road to the landing at Lowry Lake, and it is possible to park there and avoid going through the private hunt club.

Use Entrance Three, on the northwest side of SR-21, between Keystone Heights and Gold Head Branch State Park.

CAMP BRANCH CONSERVATION AREA/SAUNDERS TRACT
(Hamilton County, 200 acres, bicycling and hiking)

Like many excellent trails on Suwannee River Water Management District lands, this 6-mile trail begins with ravines, passes sinkholes, and ends at the banks of the Suwannee. Along the way, it passes through a community of active, large gopher tortoise burrows. A section of the Florida Trail passes close to a primitive camping site.

From I-75, exit to White Springs, go north on US-41, then abruptly west on CR-25A. Once

Top: **sunset over Lowry Lake at Camp Blanding.**

CR-25A crosses I-75 again, be alert after a sharp right hand turn. The entrance is merely an easement onto water management land, between Camp Branch Road and a private gate. It is almost directly behind a truck inspection station on I-75. *Managed by: Suwannee River Water Mangement District.*

LEAVE NOTHING BUT TRACKS.

It is very sad that many natural areas are littered with trash. This condition is not unique to Florida, but a large population and heavy tourism magnify the problem. Many responsible trail users backpack a trash bag, but there are obviously more ill-mannered, inconsiderate, and just uninformed people who do not understand what they are doing. Some of our discards endanger wildlife, like the ensnaring plastic rings that hold soda cans together. Some waste items, such as used diapers, may be a threat to health. Carelessly discarded garbage reduces the pleasure of the wilderness experience. Broken bottles never decompose. A beer bottle dropped in a stream could cut the toes of a child many years later. The Florida Trail Association and the agencies responsible for public lands promote a simple motto: "Take nothing but pictures, leave nothing but tracks."

CARY STATE FOREST
(Duval and Nassau counties, 3,412 acres, multi-use)

The 16 miles of multi-use roads within Cary are popular for horse riding. However, horses are not allowed on the 1-mile nature trail that includes a boardwalk through a cypress swamp. Nor are they allowed on the 5-mile hiking loop. Check in at the kiosk or forest office and receive directions on arrival. Basically this is forest with marsh and swamp. Seepage areas have hooded pitcher plants. Located on the east side of US-301, 7 miles north of US-90 and I-10 at Baldwin. *Managed by: Division of Forestry.*

CEDAR KEY SCRUB STATE RESERVE
(Levy County, 4,720 acres, multi-use)

Traveling from city to town in Florida (and the US for that matter), it is easy to get a sense of *deja vu*—the same fast food restaurants, super markets, drug stores, and gas stations. Remarkably, all the natural areas in this book differ from each other in some way.

The scrub at Cedar Key differs from the scrub on the Central Ridge, or in other coastal areas. Many typical scrub plants are here, such as gopher apple, sparkleberry, climbing buckthorn, staggerbush.

Scrub-jays can be seen, along with hundreds of other birds in the course of a year, including bald eagles and osprey. The scrub-jay population is in decline in the reserve. The mammals at this site include a fairly large feral pig population, hunted during season. Bobcats, gray foxes, and red foxes are present.

Eleven miles of multi-use trails are on dirt and grassy roads. The major communities are flatwoods, saltmarsh, and scrub dominated with sand pine and overwhelmingly conspicuous Florida rosemary.

There are trailheads on SR-24 and CR-347. Both SR-24 and CR-347 can be reached from US-19 south of Chiefland by turning west. For horse rides, management suggests the trailhead on CR-347.

CARAVELLE WILDLIFE MANAGEMENT AREA
(Marion and Putnam counties, 14,000+ acres, multi-use)

Perhaps because it is so close to the many recreational opportunities in the Ocala National Forest, this wild and lonely land gets little recreational use. It is defined by the Cross-Florida Greenway and Barge Canal to the north, Rodman Dam/Ocklawaha Recreation Area to the west, and the confluence of the Ocklawaha and St. Johns rivers.

The ten miles of multi-use, gravel and earth roads are closed to recreational use during hunting season. Some of the land was formerly cleared. Roads and trails are firm for bicycling, with no obvious blazing and several crossing trails. Camping is permitted both during and out of hunting season, with restrictions and by permit. This land is jointly owned by the state and the water management district.

There are two entrances south of Palatka on the east side of SR-19, at 1 and 2 miles south of the Cross-Florida Barge Canal. The southern entrance is wet forest and floodplain. The northern trail is through former pasture until it reaches forest and floodplain. Bald eagles nest here, and bears are sometimes seen.

Managed by: Florida Fish and Wildlife Conservation Commission and St. Johns River Water Management District.

Top: **wild azalea, usually found around river banks and swamp.**

FLORIDA'S GOPHER TORTOISE

The gopher tortoise is a creature which is able to adapt to humans. If you don't mind sacrificing a few flowers, they might dig a burrow in your yard, and otherwise be perfect house guests. Slow, ponderous, gentle vegetarians, gophers make burrows which provide shelter to more than 300 species of living things. Their presence is part of a healthy, normal Florida environment.

With human population expansion and consequent development, the tortoise is now besieged. It is often paved over and buried alive during road and home construction, despite recent laws and regulations to protect it. When displaced, it becomes vulnerable to cars and to the few animals which prey on it.

Since 1986, perhaps 36,000 Florida gopher tortoises have been destroyed by development. According to the Nature Conservancy, gophers are one of more than 570 species in danger in Florida.

PC

CROSS FLORIDA GREENWAY
(Citrus, Levy, Marion, and Putnam counties, multi-use)

The Greenway is a concept, much like the Florida Trail or rails-to-trails. It consists of interconnected areas devoted to preservation and recreation. Its path lies on lands that were at one time destined to be the Cross Florida Barge Canal, a project that would have bisected the state coast-to-coast, from the St. Johns to the Gulf of Mexico, had it not been stopped after a lengthy political battle.

Greenway trails can be seen from several tall bridges constructed in association with the canal. These include the bridges on US-19 and SR-19. From the tops of these bridges, parts of the Greenway appear along both banks receding into the distance. The section from US-19 is relatively short before it is interrupted by privately held lands, but the section seen from SR-19 goes on for a few miles. Other portions of the Greenway are less obvious, and meander through lands like the Marshall Swamp, near Silver Springs.

Like many 20th Century engineering projects, the Barge Canal was ill-conceived, and would have damaged the flow of the aquifer from north to south, while many beautiful wilderness areas would have been permanently changed. One river that was changed was the Ocklawaha, one of Florida's loveliest.

The project was begun during the depression, when men and mules carted considerable amounts of sand in wooded areas along the Greenway trails. The more obvious dredging along highways and the Ocklawaha River was done in the 1960s. Although President Nixon stopped the project, allegedly because of cost overruns, it was mostly the efforts of an extraordinary naturalist, Marjorie Harris Carr, that galvanized opposition to the project.

The 110-mile Greenway is not complete, and there is an ongoing effort to acquire land to eliminate the breaks. The Greenway sometimes is described in two sections, east and west, usually meaning east or west of I-75. Since an overpass was built, this distinction may have less and less relevance.

Rock pits dug, but never filled, provide interesting bicycling at the Santos Trailhead. It is off Southeast 80th Street in Ocala, and is the trailhead for both the east and west Florida Trail segments. The two Florida Trail segments are joined by two roads and exceed 72.5 miles.

Managed by: Ocala Field Office, Office of the Greenways

MW-SI

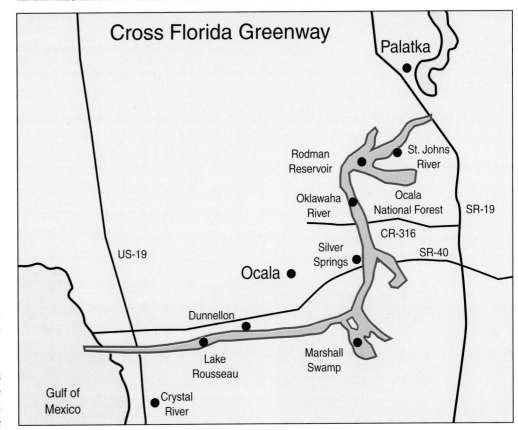

Top, left: a view of the Cross Florida Greenway from the bridge on SR-19. The channel is a section of the ill-fated Cross Florida Barge Canal.

Top, right: the Santos Trailhead of the Cross Florida Greenway is an excellent path for mountain biking.

CYPRESS CREEK CONSERVATION AREA
(Hamilton County, 1,349 acres, bicycling and hiking)

The conservation area has two tracts: Cypress Creek Wildlife Management Area and Cypress Creek South Tract. They are situated along the west bank of the Suwannee River only a few miles from Georgia. The river normally flows slower here before the major confluence with the Withlacoochee, and is not very wide at this point.

Unmarked trails extend a considerable distance along the river banks with great views of the river. Roads are firm, and biking and hiking are allowed. This is a remote and lonely place, and no one is likely to come along to offer a hand in case of an emergency.

From I-75, take SR-6 through Jasper, then turn north at CR-135 just before the Suwannee River. Across the river are the Benton Tract to the north and the Bay Creek Tract to the south. All are equally solitary experiences.

Managed by: Suwannee River Water Management District.

DELEON SPRINGS STATE RECREATION AREA
(Volusia County, 600 acres, hiking)

The springs pour forth an average 19 million gallons a day into the St. Johns River. This is a popular swimming area with an excellent canoe trip. On land, the Wild Persimmon Trail is a Florida Trail loop. The recreation area is across the lake from Lake Woodruff National Wildlife Refuge. DeLeon has 4.4 miles of hiking, the refuge has over 6 miles, and the two can be combined into one long day trip, including canoeing, hiking, and nature study. Birding is excellent during the migratory seasons. Major habitats: floodplain, hardwood hammock, lake, river, and springs. In DeLeon Springs, on SR-17, 5 miles north of Deland.

DEPOT TRAIL
(Alachua County)

This is a 2-mile, paved rail-to-trail in Gainesville. It begins at the Shands Hospital and crosses US-441. See Waldo Trail.

Managed by City of Gainesville.

TRAILWALKER TO TRAILMASTER.

This is an achievement program encouraging use of forest trails. Someone who has completed ten trails is a Trailwalker, 20 trails a Trailblazer, and 30 trails a Trailmaster. Most of the forests in the program have kiosks where forms can be completed once the trail is hiked, then sent to Division of Forestry. Sometimes these supplies are depleted, and it may be necessary to contact a forest office, or the Division of Forestry directly.

DUNNS CREEK CONSERVATION AREA
(Putnam County, 3,182 acres, multi-use)

This is mostly wetlands or floodplain along Dunns Creek and Crescent Lake. Its wet condition is indicated by the names Long Swamp, Moccasin Landing, and Sykes Landing. As would be expected, the floodplain contains both cypress and hardwoods, while the uplands are pine and mixed forest. There are approximately 4 miles of multi-use trails (4 in/4 out) and a small loop. There are two difficult-to-find trailheads off SR-100 to the southeast of Palatka. The first trailhead is on Tram Road, and the other is on San Mateo Cemetery Road.

Managed by: St. Johns River Water Management District.

Top: cypress along the Sante Fe River, a tributary of the Suwannee River.
Bottom, left: a hiker along the Suwannnee River in the Cypress Creek Conservation Area.
Above: a bright red amanita mushroom.

EMERALDA MARSH CONSERVATION AREA
(Lake County, 7089 acres. multi-use)

Between lakes Griffin and Yale, this beautiful conservation area is mostly water. The National Park Service designated this area a National Natural Landmark.

Many unblazed miles of equestrian and hiking trails wind around the lake shore and marsh, where wading birds and alligators are easy to spot, and an osprey might swoop overhead. Sandhill cranes winter here. Primitive camping is available at designated sites.

It is rather remarkable that so attractive a place, and a natural landmark, is barely used for recreation or nature observation. Perhaps this has to do with its comparatively remote location. Habitats: oak and palm dominated hammock, lake, and marsh, with scattered pines.

Between SR-42 and SR-44, it is reached from CR-452 south of the Ocala National Forest. A loop between the towns of Emeralda to the north and Lisbon to the south can be driven by following CR-452 and Emeralda Island Road. There are trailheads along the east and west sides of this loop—at least three on CR-452, and four or more on Emeralda Island Road.

Managed by: St. Johns River Water Management District.

ETONIAH CREEK STATE FOREST
(Putnam County, 8,604 acres, multi-use)

While the forest contains longleaf pine, there is plentiful scrub dominated by sand pine. There is a 4.75-mile hiking trail and many miles of multi-use roads, but bicycling might be laborious due to the sandy conditions. The namesake, Etoniah Creek, is a pretty little stream.

The Division of Forestry encourages individuals to become "Trailwalkers." Thus, this trail to the north of SR-100 in Florahome is announced by a sign reading "Trailwalker," 16 miles to the west of Palatka, with an arrow indicating the way north to the trailhead.

Information on the Trailwalker Program is available from the Division of Forestry.

FLAT ISLAND PRESERVE
(Lake County, 2300+ acres, hiking)

Maintained by the Florida Trail Association, the Daubenmire Trail is a excellent path through hardwood forest and past the wetlands of the Okahumpka Marsh. The marsh waters flow into Lake Denham and Lake Harris. The trail is a 3-mile loop with an entry trail and side trails for additional distance. There is also a 440-foot boardwalk. A laminated map of the trail is available through the Florida Trail Association. It is possible, with coordination with Lake County Water Authority, to use canoes on the property to paddle to Magnolia Island. There are plans to expand trails in the preserve, and facilities and trails on the island. There is limited camping by permit.

South of Leesburg, from US-27, turn west on CR-25A. There are prominent signs with directions to the preserve. CR-25A pops out again farther north on US-27, but this is quite

some distance from the preserve. The building at the trailhead is not an office, but a private residence.

Managed by: Lake County Water Authority.

FANNING SPRINGS STATE RECREATION AREA/NATURE COAST STATE TRAIL
(Levy County, bicycling and hiking)

This popular, small recreation area has been best known for its two attractive springs: Big and Little Fanning. Big Fanning is one of Florida's 27 first-magnitude springs. In addition, there is also a short, pretty trail through pines and hardwood. This recreation area is next door to the Nature Coast State Trail, an expanding rail-to-trail, including a Suwannee River crossing over the old railroad bridge. 32 paved miles are planned. Some maps show the trail passing through the wildlife management areas along the Gulf Coast. At present, this is fanciful, but perhaps at some future date it might happen. Those areas have a mixed variety of paved, dirt, and sand roads. Biking through the sand requires tri-athlete strength. However, those trips can be rewarded both by isolation and beautiful glimpses of the Gulf. Fanning Springs is on US-19, south of the Suwannee River, on the west side of the road. The trail is across US-19 opposite the recreation area.

FOX TRAIL TRACT
(Suwannee County, 188 acres, bicycling and hiking)

This is a delightful small tract within the Fort Union Conservation Area. It has 1.63 miles of Suwannee River frontage and trails. The easy part of the directions are to take US-129 north for 7 miles from Live Oak, then go west for 3 miles on CR-132. Sometimes the next two signs are down. Go north on CR-795 a short ways, then turn onto a dirt road known as 24th Street. The entrance is off 107th Road to the left.

Managed by: Suwannee River Water Management District.

Top: a bridge across the Suwannee River on the Nature Coast Trail.
Bottom: ironweed among ferns. Ironweed grows in sandhill and dry flatwoods.

PC

FT. CLINCH STATE PARK
(Nassau County, 1,100 acres, bicycling and hiking)

A fort from the Civil War, it stands on the northeast end of Fernandina Beach, its impressive but silent cannons still overlooking Cumberland Island, Georgia, the St. Marys River, and the Atlantic Ocean. Hiking and bicycling are on 6.5 miles of trail alongside the coastal saltmarsh and the Atlantic beaches. The 3.5 miles of roads, most paved, are very popular for bicycling. Other habitats include dune and scrub, and there are over 2 miles of beautiful beach to walk. Colorful flowers adorn the beach and the areas between the dunes. This is a very well organized park with camping facilities. From A1A in Fernandina, follow the signs north.

FT. GEORGE ISLAND STATE PARK
See Talbot GeoPark

PC

PC

Top: a pondweed-covered marsh beside the trail at Ft. Clinch State Park.

Above: guns from the Civil War stand silently at Ft. Clinch State Park.

Bottom, left: holly grows wild along trails adjoining the marshes at Ft. Clinch State Park. Eleven kinds of holly can be found in Florida. One holly is yaupon. Another, tawnberry, is found only in Dade County. The most widespread is probably American holly. All hollys have colorful berries.

GAINESVILLE-HAWTHORNE STATE TRAIL
(Alachua County, multi-use)

This rail-to-trail connects Gainesville to Hawthorne 15 miles to the east. There is a parallel equestrian trail. From Hawthorne, the trail appears uncompromisingly straight until near Paynes Prairie State Preserve. Just before the Preserve, where the trail bends, there is a floodplain that contains an unusual mix of cypress and pines. The trail continues into the Preserve along rolling hills and by deep sinks. Here the trail is a favorite of fast-moving, healthy-looking University of Florida co-eds on bicycles and roller blades.

Terminus in Gainesville: exit I-75 at Williston Road (SR-331), go east for 4.2 miles, then turn right on SE 4th Street, and right again at SE 15th Street, then go .6 miles to Boulware Springs Park on the right side of the road. The terminus in Hawthorne is near the intersection of US-301 and SR-20 and is exceptionally well-marked. The Gainesville terminus is difficult to find.

Managed by: Paynes Prairie State Preserve.

Top, left: the straightness of Gainesville-Hawthorne State Trail is evident in this photo.

Top, right: one of the bridges crossing creeks along Gainesville-Hawthorne StateTrail.

Center: a bicyclist takes a break from pedalling Gainesville-Hawthorne State Trail.

Right: cypress and cypress knees in a flooded area of Goethe State Forest.

GAR POND TRACT
(Hamilton County, 521 acres, bicycling and hiking)

Gar Pond is a tract of the Suwannee Valley Conservation Area. Approximately 6 miles of trails wind through the flatwoods around Gar Pond. The trails are popular with local hikers and mountain bike riders. Located on the west side of US-41, a mile or so south of White Springs. *Managed by: Suwannee River Water Management District.*

GOETHE STATE FOREST
(Levy County, 50,171 acres, multi-use)

Although primarily a longleaf pine forest, with flatwoods and sandhill, there are over 15 natural communities within the forest, including hardwood hammock and cypress swamp.

Within Goethe are many limerock roads suitable for vehicles. The roads, and most of the trails, are sufficiently compact to support bicycles. Goethe is multi-use, open also to equestrian riders and hikers. Overnight camping is possible with a permit.

The Division of Forestry lists two trails within the "Trailwalker Program," each up to 10 miles in length: Tidewater and Black Prong. Daniels Trail is listed at 15 miles. The Apex Trail includes a number of connectors, loops, and trails, and appears to be almost 24 miles. Forest representatives say there are are a total of 100 miles of trail.

Goethe has a population of red-cockaded woodpeckers. Flora includes coontie and pitcher plants. Black bears are sometimes seen, and Sherman's fox squirrels are easy to spot.

Forest location: the forest lies to the east of US-19 from Lebanon Station. It is north of SR-40, and west of CR-336. CR-336 and CR-337 have the trailheads. A map is available from the forest headquarters.

Managed by: Division of Forestry.

GOLD HEAD BRANCH STATE PARK
(Clay County, 2100 acres, bicycling and hiking)

At Gold Head Branch State Park, you can visit the third oldest Florida lake. The still, dark waters of Lake Sheelar, and the shore around it, indeed appear as something from the distant past, surrounded by scrub plants and Florida rosemary, as it undoubtedly has been for eons.

The older lakes in Florida are Lake Annie and Lake Tulane in Highlands County. They are thought to be over 30,000 years old. Comparatively, the Everglades and Lake Okeechobee may be less than one third that age. Some sediments in Lake Sheelar have been dated and found to be around 23,500 years old.

Bicycling is allowed on the roads; however note they can be busy roads. The Florida Trail passing through Gold Head Branch is 3 miles long. The Loblolly and Ravines trails are 1.25 miles together. The Ravines Trail, with short bridges across trickling Gold Head Branch, is an exceptional trail. The ravines were created by spring water flowing over many millennia toward Lake Johnson, where swimming is now a popular activity.

Cabins and camping, including primitive style, are available at Gold Head. Habitats: lakes, ravine, sandhill, and scrub.

Located on SR-21, six miles northeast of Keystone Heights.

Top, left: autumn at Gold Head Branch State Park.

Top, right: the scrub around Lake Sheelar on a foggy morning.

Above: the seeds of a milkweed plant.

Bottom, left: deer tracks in the sand. Deer tracks are easy to recognize because there are only two grooves and the tracks are usually very deep.

Bottom, right: brilliant flowers of butterfly weed.

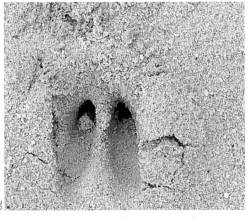

Opposite page, top: Gold Head Branch running through the ravine at Gold Head Branch State Park.

Opposite page, bottom: looking down the incline of the ravines, Gold Head Branch State Park.

37

GUANA RIVER STATE PARK/ WILDLIFE MANAGEMENT AREA
(St. Johns County, 12,035 acres, bicycling and hiking)

Bicycle and hiking trails within the park are in 5 loops and total 9.6 miles. They pass through forest, both pines and hardwoods, by scenic marsh, and along the Talamato River, part of the Intracoastal Waterway. At 9,815 acres, the adjacent wildlife management area is the larger of the two public lands, and a lengthy combination of road, unimproved road, and trail run through it.

The state park lies on both sides of A1A between sand dunes, and has beach parking for those who wish to enjoy a 4-mile stretch of undisturbed Atlantic beach. Some dunes reach 40 feet in height. Bicycles and beach can be combined to create a greater weekend adventure.

Along A1A, south of Jacksonville and north of St. Augustine.

Managed by: Florida Fish and Wildlife Conservation Commission.

GUM ROOT PARK/GUM ROOT SWAMP CONSERVATION AREA
(Alachua County, 741 acres, bicycling and hiking)

A short hike of perhaps a mile through the conservation area leads to a heart-warming sight. Stand among the large cypress by its shores and look out at Newmans Lake. It offers a breathtaking vista of undeveloped, unmarred shoreline. Many Florida lakes have had their natural splendor ruined by encroaching development, whether fancy upscale homes, or dismal looking fishing camps.

Gum Root offers 4 miles of mountain biking and hiking. The trail on the north side of SR-26 goes mostly through woods and is perhaps 2.5 miles in length. The south side has a shorter trail, but it is more scenic and leads to Newmans Lake, passing over boardwalks along the way.

Located on both sides of SR-26, 5 miles east of Gainesville.

Managed by: The City of Gainesville and the St. Johns River Water Management District.

Top: lightning from a thunderstorm over Newmans Lake at Gum Root Swamp Conservation Area.

Bottom: a bicyclist enjoying a rare straight ahead on the trail in Guana River State Park.

3,000 YEARS AGO AT NEWNANS LAKE

During the prolonged drought of 2000, when Newnans Lake was 5 feet lower than normal, the remains of more than 20 canoes were found, some as old as 3,000 years. Prehistoric Native Americans probably used them to *fish. The canoes were as long as 22 feet, and showed signs of having been made by scraping and burning. Native Americans came to Florida probably between 10-12,000 years ago.*

(KATHYRN ABBEY) HANNA PARK
(Duval County, 450 acres, bicycling and hiking).

With 1.5 miles of beach and dunes, a 7-mile bicycling and hiking trail, and a shorter 1-mile trail near a campground, this is an exceptionally popular recreation area. The paved road into the park is 1.5 miles and can be bicycled. From Jacksonville, take SR-10 east 13 miles to A1A north and follow the signs.
Managed by: City of Jacksonville.

HEART ISLAND CONSERVATION AREA
(Volusia County, 11,112 acres, multi-use)

This land was recovering from clear-cutting in 1994, and was being restored largely with longleaf pine when a wildfire devastated the area in 1998. Restoration was set back, but is underway once again. By 2000, most of the area had recovered. Habitats: flatwoods, floodplain, hardwood hammock, scrub, streams, and swamp. The trails are multi-use roads and footpaths.

This area is east of Ocala National Forest. There are two trailheads on the south side of SR-40. Farther east, turning north on SR-11, leads to another trailhead on the west side of the road.
Managed by: St. Johns River Water Management District.

HOLTON CREEK CONSERVATION AREA
(Hamilton County, 2,531 acres, multi-use)

This unit contains a 16-mile portion of the Florida Trail for hiking only. Bicycling is allowed on the roads. The area is also very popular for equestrian use because there are long, scenic rides. Primitive camping is available, but only out of hunting season with permit. It is a gorgeous area of cypress and hardwoods. Habitats include forest, sinkholes, and cypress swamp.

From Live Oak, take SR-249 north approximately 12 miles. Turn east on Adams Grade Road about .5 miles north of the Suwannee River bridge. *Managed by: Suwannee River Water Management District.*

Top: the dunes at Hanna Park.

Bottom: gorgeous natural scenery along Holton Creek.

PETS IN THE PARKS

The following state forests, parks, and recreation areas in this book presently allow pets in campgrounds: Blackwater River, Blue Spring, Collier-Seminole, Florida Caverns, Fort Clinch, Gold Head Branch, Highlands Hammock, Hillsborough River, Jonathan Dickinson, Lake Manatee, Little Manatee River, Manatee Springs, Ochlockonee River, Oscar Scherer, Rocky Bayou, St. George Island, Stephen Foster, Suwannee River, Talbot GEO Park, Three Rivers, Tomoka, Topsail Hill, and Wekiwa Springs. This follows a growing trend recognizing the value of pets to their owners. Some areas in this book allow pets to be walked on certain trails, but it is always best to check about pets.

Pets are often not allowed on the trails, and never on public beaches or in picnic areas. When pets are allowed on trails, owners should consider the safety of the animal and the convenience of other recreational users. Pets need to be kept on leashes, and even then caution should be used. There is no anticipating how a domestic animal, no matter how well-behaved, will react when meeting wild animals. Dogs also can become targets of alligators.

ICHETUCKNEE SPRINGS STATE PARK
(Suwannee County, 2,300 acres)

The portion of the hiking trail along the incredible Ichetucknee River will remain in memory long after the visit is over. Pure spring water rushes out at the river head. The waters look invitingly aqua against the sand bottom and vegetated floodplain.

Ichetucknee is best known for its tubing, although in cooler months, it is a splendid canoe journey. Tubing and swimming in the summer months is multi-culture, multi-gender, multi-generation, and multitudinous. Ichetucknee is a wonderful place, full of the magic of the outdoors, where large groups of people get along and have fun together. On some weekends in summer, the parking lots are closed because the crowds might damage the river. The biggest threat to Ichetucknee, aside from the incinerator mentioned on this page, is being loved to death by too many people.

The park is management for Troy Springs State Park, 5 miles northwest of Branford on the Suwannee River. This small park presently can only be reached by boat. There are plans to make this area more open to the public.

There are two entrances near Ft. White to Ichetucknee. The northern entrance is on CR-238. There is a hiking trail there with two loops, Pine Ridge and Trestle Point. These total 2.25 miles. The southern entrance is on US-27. There is a trail at the southern entrance that parallels the river for about 0.75 miles.

Top: floodplain along the Ichetucknee River.
Bottom: the confluence of the Ichetucknee and Sante Fe rivers.
Opposite page, top, left and right: the Ichetucknee River, with and without the summer tubing crowd.
Opposite page, bottom: Mystery Spring Run in Ichetucknee State Park.

THE ICHETUCKNEE INCINERATOR

A cement plant under construction near the Ichetucknee has ignited an environmental firestorm. The plant will have an incinerator that burns, among other things, tires. Not only is there fear that the aroma of burning tires and ash will fill the pure air around Ichetucknee. All incinerators put out mercury and nitrates, among other things. Some mercury seems bound to fall into the Ichetucknee, which flows into the Sante Fe, which flows into the Suwannee, which flows into the Gulf of Mexico. Further, nitrates enrich the waters, perhaps resulting in unplanned consequences. The State Department of Environmental Protection first turned down the plant because the parent company of the cement plant had a controversial past. When the public furor died down, DEP reversed itself and approved the plant, saying it had met all legal standards.

Further complicated dealings involve purchasing a mining operation of the parent company to shut it down. It is safe to say that many Floridians are very unhappy not only with the cement plant proceeding, but also with DEP's apparent flip-flop.

Although there must be a place for incinerators, the question is, why here, next to a natural wonder.

FLOODPLAIN

Floodplain is a very common ecosystem or habitat. Where rivers overflow their banks, rich deposits of soil accumulate, promoting the growth of plants and trees. These places are often dark and dense with vegetation. Some floodplains stretch far away from the river, or in many cases, occupy land between the forks of a river. Gorgeous flood-plain exists in many areas of Florida. In addition to the Ichetucknee, three examples of rivers with scenic floodplains are the Apalachicola, Chipola, and Hillsborough. The plants and trees growing in a floodplain receive some fire protection because floodplain is often damp or flooded. Fire is a prime influence on habitat, because some tree species, especially some pines, are more fire resistant than others. In a forest where fire has favored pines by eliminating their competition, one can sometimes see in the distance a line of oaks indicating the path of a river with its adjacent floodplain. Trees commonly seen in floodplain are oaks, tupelos, gums, cypress, and palms.

Opposite page, top: climbing aster is a common, colorful sight along Florida rivers, especially in fall.
Opposite page, bottom left: a very large live oak in the Sante Fe River floodplain. This oak has a circumference of 23 feet.
Opposite page, bottom right: the base of a large cypress in the Sante Fe River
Top: profuse atamasco lilies are a common sight in floodplain areas.
Bottom: a hiker on a fall stroll at Ichetucknee Springs State Park.

JACKSONVILLE-BALDWIN TRAIL
(Duval County, bicycling and hiking, equestrian planned)

This 14.5-mile rail-to-trail passes through suburbia, and past businesses and commercial lumbering to the west of Jacksonville. The trail opened in November 1999, and it is perfect for biking, blading, or hiking. While an equestrian trail is planned, no completion date has yet been given. The Baldwin Trailhead is in the town of Baldwin on CR-121, north of US-90 and I-10. The Jacksonville Trailhead is west of I-295 on Imeson Road in Jacksonville. *Managed by: City of Jacksonville.*

RAILS-TO-TRAILS CONSERVANCY

A non-profit organization supporting the conservation of former rail trails for recreational activities, the Rails-to-Trails Conservancy has a Florida office. Their address is 2545 Blairstone Pines Drive, Tallahassee, Florida 32301. Phone: 850-942-2379. Fax: 850-942-4431. A guide to Florida Rail-to-Trails is available from this organization at a reasonable charge. It contains detailed maps for over 20 rail-to-trails. By coincidence, David Gluckman, the author of that guide, is shown in the photo at the top of this page riding the Jacksonville-Baldwin Trail on its opening day.

THE PLANT TO BE AVOIDED

Poison ivy is a plant that occurs over much of the eastern US, and Florida is no exception. In Florida, it is primarily found in woodlands and in disturbed areas. Usually found either growing close to the ground or climbing trees, it can be recognized by the three distinguishing leaflets and the small, clustered white fruits. Sensitive individuals often blister badly and have severe itching and skin irritation. Lotions may soothe the irritation, but poison ivy is best avoided.

JENNINGS STATE FOREST
(Clay County, 20,623 acres, multi-use)

This forest has a great diversity of habitats including flatwoods, ravines, sandhill, swamp, and streams. Two rare plants found in Jennings are Bartram's ixia and St. John's Susan.

The most scenic area is along Black Creek. This tributary of the St. Johns is the same river that flows through the Black Creek Conservation Area. Portions are outstanding Florida canoe trails.

The North Fork Black Creek Trail can be 18 miles, but it is possible to take short-cuts on crossing roads. The Fire and Water Nature Trail is approximately 0.75 miles. Bicycle riding would be a nightmare in places due to the deep "sugar" sand, yet this is a multi-use area. The horse trails are actively used by local residents. Primitive camping is available.

There are five entrances into Jennings, but the recreational trails are best reached from one. From I-10 at Baldwin, take US-301 south approximately 10.5 miles to CR-218, then go east on CR-218 to SR-121 in Middleburg. Go north on SR-121 about 1.5 miles. After crossing Black Creek Bridge, turn left onto Long Bay Road, then left onto Old Jennings Road, and right on Live Oak Lane. Follow it to the trailheads on left side of the road. *Managed by: Division of Forestry and St. Johns River W.M.D.*

Above, left: bicycle enthusiasts on the opening day of the Jacksonville-Baldwin Trail.
Above, right: jack-in-the-pulpit is found in floodplain areas.
Below: two local residents who ride the trails in Jennings State Forest almost every day.
Opposite page, top: Adam's needle is found in scrub and pine flatwoods.

LAKE BUTLER WILDLIFE MANAGEMENT AREA
(Baker and Union counties, 31,000+ acres, multi-use)

South of Osceola National Forest, this wildlife area is a pine plantation of the Georgia-Pacific Corporation. Multi-use is not allowed on the Florida Trail portion. The Florida Trailheads are at the Olustee Battlefield State Historic Site on US-90 and on the east side of CR-231, 1 mile north of SR-100, southeast of Lake City. *Managed by: Florida Fish and Wildlife Conservation Commission.*

LAKE GEORGE CONSERVATION AREA
(Volusia County, 19,831 acres, multi-use)

This conservation area helps protect the east shore and watershed of Florida's second largest lake. (In order, Florida's five largest lakes are: Okeechobee, George, Kissimmee, Apopka, and Istokpoga. In reality, nothing comes close to Okeechobee. Lake George is little more than one-tenth the size of Lake Okeechobee). The conservation area is jointly owned by the county and state. There are more than 10 miles of multi-use trail. Habitats: floodplain, flatwoods, lake, and swamp. From US-17, go south 9 miles from Crescent City, then go west on CR-305 (Lake George Drive) at the town of Seville. *Managed by: St. Johns River Water Management District.*

LAKE MONROE CONSERVATION AREA
(Seminole and Volusia counties, 7,390 acres, multi-use)

Most of this area is Lake Monroe floodplain with cypress and hardwoods. There is a multi-use loop trail of approximately 3 to 4 miles. Primitive camping is available at designated sites. Take CR-415 east from Sanford. CR-415 splits. There is parking north on Reed Ellis Road. There is a 2-mile loop trail, and a slightly longer deadend to the river in this half of the conservation area designated the Kratzert Tract. The other half of the area is south of CR-415, and known as the Brickyard Slough Tract. It has a 3-mile loop. (Note that at least one guidebook identifies CR-415 as SR-415). *Managed by: St. Johns Water Management District.*

LAKE WOODRUFF NATIONAL WILDLIFE REFUGE
(Volusia County, 22,000 acres, bicycling and hiking)

The lake, marsh, streams, and swamp here have been altered by canals and dikes. It is possible to hike on the levees as part of the 6-mile hiking trail. All areas within the refuge are open for bicycle riding, but no equestrian use is allowed. There is also a shorter nature trail. This is an excellent place to see water birds during the migratory months. Portions of the trail on the dikes are shadeless. From US-17, go northwest of Deland on CR-4053. Go left on Mud Lake Road to the parking areas. Canoe access is off SR-44.

LITTLE TALBOT ISLAND STATE PARK.
See Talbot GeoPark

LOCHLOOSA CONSERVATION AREA
(Alachua County, 27,327 acres, multi-use)

Some of this land borders Lochloosa Lake, and includes forested land, flatwoods, hardwoods, marsh, and swamp. A smaller portion has shoreline on Orange Lake. In this area, bald eagles, sandhill cranes, and wood storks are frequently seen. Florida black bear can also sometimes be seen briefly.

Most trails are along more than 20 miles of roads, sometimes open for vehicles. Some unblazed trails loop from the roads. All are multi-use, but most mortal bicyclists will quickly grind to an abrupt stop in sandy stretches. Primitive camping is available, but not during hunting season.

Maps are certainly helpful. They can be obtained from the Florida Fish and Wildlife Conservation Commission. A map is also included in the St. Johns River Water Management District Recreational Guide. Both are free, and can be obtained from addresses in the Appendix and on the internet.

There are several entrances. One popular entrance with an observation deck is in Cross Creek, made famous by the author and environmentalist, Marjorie Kinnan Rawlings; that entrance is next to the fire station on CR-325, south from SR-20 or west from US-301. The deck overlooks a marshy portion of the lake.

Another popular entrance is beside the Gainesville-Hawthorne State Trail, near Hawthorne, off CR-2082, which runs between CR-325 and US-301.

Managed by: St. Johns River Water Management District.

Top: a fallen and bleached tree lies among needlerush and saltwort in Lower Suwannee National Wildlife Refuge.

Bottom: a very young loggerhead musk turtle from the Sante Fe River.

LOWER SUWANNEE NATIONAL WILDLIFE REFUGE
(Dixie and Levy counties, 52,935 acres, bicycling and hiking)

The main refuge road (Loop Road) is 9 miles long and can be pedaled, driven by car, or hiked. Horses are not allowed in the refuge.

Loop Road has two entrances, the south and north gates, open round the clock. Numerous dirt roads and paths depart from it for the adventuresome and curious, adding many additional miles. A very short River Trail is located near the headquarters, and there are two trails which total 1.3 miles at the Shell Mound Unit. Levy County maintains a camping area at Shell Mound, and Dixie County has one at the end of CR-357.

The 29,000 refuge acres in Dixie County are best accessed from CR-349 and CR-357. There is a scenic, 9-mile road through coastal wetlands and bottom land hardwoods. It starts near the town of Suwannee on CR-349 and ends at beautiful Shired Island on CR-357. Observation towers are located at Fishbone and Salt creeks.

The refuge has excellent canoe and kayak trails. With the Cedar Key National Wildlife Refuge in the Gulf, and Waccasassa Bay Preserve to the south, the paddling can be endless. The Cedar Key refuge includes several unspoiled barrier islands. If exploring by water, watch the tides carefully, because this area is shallow and stranding can be a problem at low tide.

Since the refuge includes 26 miles along the Gulf of Mexico, many miles along the Suwannee River, and significant inland acreage, there is a great variety of habitats: flatwoods, floodplain, hammock, marsh, river, saltmarsh, scrub, and swamp.

Osprey nests overlook the tidal marsh. Swallow-tailed kites and bald eagles also nest in the refuge. Deer, turtles, and turkeys are prevalent along the roads. Biting insects are numerous in the summer months. It is best to visit in winter, or take plenty of repellent.

From five miles south of Chiefland on US-19, take CR-347 west. Or take SR-24 off US-19 at Otter Creek to reach CR-347. At the Gulf end of SR-24, is Cedar Key, known for its seafood, restaurants, laid-back atmosphere, and offshore fishing.

MANATEE SPRINGS STATE PARK
(Levy County, 2,075 acres, bicycling and hiking)

There are 8.5 miles of trails in the northeastern portion of the park. These trails and the very short Sinkhole Trail (2/3 of a mile) are beneath scenic hardwoods and occasional pine. Along the Sinkhole Trail are perhaps a half dozen sinks that usually contain water. There is a magnificent boardwalk along the spring run to the Suwannee, an area with gorgeous cypress.

Manatee Springs is one of the 27 first-magnitude springs in Florida. It is partially walled-in and one of the favorite places to swim in this area, especially on hot summer weekends. The park also has a popular campground.

It is not unusual to hear visitors on the boardwalk discussing manatees and searching for them in the spring run and river. West Indian manatees do come to the spring occasionally in cold weather. The lucky visitor might be blessed with a manatee sighting, or not, but the beauty of this magnificent park is the prime attraction, not manatees.

From US-19 in Chiefland, go 6 miles west on SR-320.

Top, left: red cypress and maple changing color in the fall.

Middle, right: the spring run from Manatee Springs flows into the Suwannee River.

Bottom: two sandhill cranes sparring.

SANDHILL CRANES

Most sandhills arrive in winter and stay over into spring. They are often seen on the side of roads or in open ares, like golf courses. Among the places in this books where sandhills are prominently seen are Myakka State Park and Paynes Prairie State Preserve. They are fascinating birds to observe, and their behavior is much studied. Sandhills mate for life and produce one to two chicks at a time.

MATTAIR SPRING TRACT/
WOODS FERRY TRACT
**(Suwannee County, 1,189 acres,
1,097 acres, multi-use)**

Mattair is part of the Woods Ferry Conservation Area along the west (or in this case, because of bends, actually the south) bank of the Suwannee River. This fantastic area has 12 miles of intertwining, crossing, multi-use service road and marked trail. It is exceptional Suwannee viewing, with water-worn banks of limestone.

The Suwannee Bicycle Association hopes to improve and blaze this section, and to connect it in time to other conservation tracts.

Woods Ferry is connected by trails, but could easily be considered a separate area. It has multi-use service roads and equally great overlooks of the Suwannee. The Woods Ferry Conservation Area includes Suwannee Springs (see separate account).

From I-75, exit at White Springs on SR-136 and go west for 3 miles. Turn north on CR-136A, and take 85th Road to 75th Road. For Woods Ferry, from CR136-A, the entrance is on 57th Road. US-129 joins CR-136A north of Live Oak.

Managed by: Suwannee River Water Management District.

Top: the tannin-colored waters of the Suwannee River are flowing over sandbars during a period of low water.

Bottom: white limestone walls jut out along the Suwannee river at Mattair Springs.

MOSES CREEK
CONSERVATION AREA
(St. Johns County, 2,042 acres, multi-use)

The creek is one of the few remaining undeveloped tidal creeks in the north, and a tributary of the Mantanzas River. Habitats: flatwoods, marsh, saltmarsh, scrub, and swamp dominated by cypress. There are perhaps 8 miles of multi-use trails. Primitive camping is available beside marsh at Braddock Point in the southeast corner of the area. The entrance is 8 miles south of St. Augustine, between SR-206 and the Mantanzas River. From US-1, turn east on CR-206. Two prominent trailheads lie on the north side of the road. *Managed by: St. Johns River Water Management District.*

MOSS BLUFF RECREATION AREA
See Sunnyhill Restoration Area

NATURE COAST STATE TRAIL
See Fanning Springs State Recreation Area

Top: a beautiful waterfall is located along Falling Creek to the south of White Springs. For years it was on private property, but the land has recently been purchased by the Suwannee River Water Management District. Old trails near it were closed and the area had not yet been opened to the public as of publication date.

Bottom: resurrection fern and fungus growing on a dead trunk. Resurrection fern is so named because it seems to come back from the dead just hours after a rainfall. Although normally dull-colored, and wilted in appearance during dry spells, the plant dramatically changes to a perky bright green as shown in the photo.

OCALA NATIONAL FOREST
(Lake, Marion, and Putnam counties, 384,000 acres, multi-use)

The Ocala is perhaps the most scenic national forest in Florida, and certainly the one with the most varied recreational opportunities. It is divided into two management districts, Seminole and Lake George. The forest has a wide variety of habitats: flatwoods, floodplain, lakes, marsh, prairie, river, scrub, sinkholes, springs, and swamp, with many transition zones.

The largest sand pine forest in the world is mostly in the Lake George District, but some is in Seminole. This is the 205,000-acre Big Scrub, which is harvested for pulp.

In addition to miles of trails, there are numerous canoe journeys on many of the spring runs. A 66-mile stretch of the Florida Trail passes through both districts. The best approach to exploring this very large forest is to obtain a forest map from the district offices.

Away from busy camping areas, wildlife is abundant. This includes birds, reptiles, amphibians, and large mammals, like deer and bear. In fact, the Ocala is one of the most likely places in Florida to spot a bear.

LAKE GEORGE DISTRICT

In addition to the Florida Trail, shorter nature trails lead from the Grassy Pond, Hopkins Prairie, Juniper Springs, Lake Delancy, Salt Springs, and Silver Glen Springs recreation

sites. Within the Juniper Springs Recreation Site is Fern Hammock Springs, which, because of its beauty, has been often photographed. The 7-mile Juniper Springs Run is a very popular canoe trip. The water of Salt Springs acquired its salty taste from ancient salt deposits left during epochs of higher seas.

There are 34 miles of equestrian trails (Lake, Alachua, and Marion trails) on which hikers are frequently seen.

Lake Eaton Sink is a very large sinkhole, approximately 110 feet deep, and 450 feet wide, and has a boardwalk leading to the bottom. Hickories, oaks, and magnolias reach skyward out of the sink. The trail is 2.2 miles, however a shorter loop allows access to the sinkhole within 1 mile. It is not the largest sinkhole in the state, either in width or depth, but it is very impressive.

Top: a view from the short nature trail along Juniper Springs Run, a very popular canoe journey.

Bottom: a trail in the Big Scrub, the largest sand pine forest in the world.

Opposite page, top left: Ocala National Forest has long, scenic equestrian trials.

Opposite page, middle left: an old stone bridge spans Juniper Springs Run.

Opposite page, bottom: Fern Creek in the Juniper Springs Recreation Area of the Ocala National Forest.

THE ST. FRANCIS LOOP

The St. Francis Loop Trail is an excellent hiking trail on the southeastern edge of the Ocala National Forest. The shorter walk is around the Yellow Loop at 2.8 miles. Continuing on the Blue Trail is a 7-mile trip. This very wild place is named not for the saint of the animals, but for a small, nearby pioneer town. The trailhead is on the north side of SR-42, 2 miles west of the junction with SR-44.

SEMINOLE DISTRICT

Hiking trails diverge from the Alexander Springs, Buck Lake, Clearwater Lake, and River Forest recreation sites. The Paisley Woods Mountain Bike Trail forms a figure-8, 22 miles in length, starting from Alexander Springs. The recreation area at Alexander Springs has a boardwalk which passes through splendid hammock and along a portion of the spring run. One hundred miles of equestrian trails are within the Seminole District, including Flatwoods (40), Prairie (40), and Baptist Lake (20) trails. The bicycle and equestrian trails can also be used by hikers. Alexander Springs run is one of the best canoe journeys within the forest.

Forest Location. This is a large forest that stretches from North Florida into the central area. The forest is bisected by SR-40 from east to west, accessible from I-75 or I-95. SR-19 runs north-south through the forest. The city of Palatka is to the northeast, while Ocala is to the west. A rough southern boundary would be SR-42.

OCKLAWAHA PRAIRIE RESTORATION AREA

(Marion County, 6,077 acres, multi-use)

North of Lake Weir and south of the Ocala National Forest, this area adjoins the Cross-Florida Greenway. This land acquisition is part of the effort to restore the natural Ocklawaha floodplain. Perhaps 8 miles of multi-use trails, some one way, take the traveler through potential bear country.

The southernmost section, where there is one of two trailheads, has the unusual name of Chernobyl Memorial Forest, and was named in memory of those killed or injured during that Russian nuclear power plant accident. In October 2000, it was mostly pine plantation about five feet tall.

The Chernobyl trailhead is on the north side of CR-464. The Restoration Area trailhead is on 137th Avenue, a dirt road west of CR-314A. Both areas are south of the Ocala National Forest. CR-314A connects to SR-40 in that forest and also runs into CR-464.

O'LENO STATE PARK/RIVER RISE STATE PRESERVE

(Columbia and Alachua counties, 6,000 acres, multi-use)

The Sante Fe River flows into O'Leno only to disappear underground at River Sink. Part of it backs-up into Ogden Lake, and the rest continues underground to reappear in River Rise State Preserve 3 miles away. The Sante Fe is a 76-mile, spring-fed river, originating in Putnam County, and is a tributary of the Suwannee.

Within O'Leno, the River Trail is one of Florida's finest walks, with turtles seemingly on every log, and deer common. The Limestone Trail near the entrance is the only trail that does not cross or connect with the others. Horseback riding is allowed south of Bellamy Road in what is River Rise Preserve. O'Leno has stabling for 20 horses, available on a first come, first served basis.

Bicycling and Hiking: Bellamy Road, 5 miles one way. Limestone Trail, 1 mile. Old Wire Road, 2.5 miles, one way. Pareners Branch Loop, 3.5 miles. River Trail, 2 miles. **Equestrian:** 13-15 miles.

Take I-75 High Springs exit west and proceed on US-41/441. There are two High Springs exits. From the southernmost, travel northwest on US-441. From the northern, travel south.

Top: Ogden Lake in O'Leno State Park.

Above: the suspension bridge in O'Leno State Park.

BEAR ENCOUNTERS

It usually lasts only a few seconds. Once the bear realizes it has been seen, it will rapidly crash off, running in a straight line over almost everything in its path. Because of the elusive nature of bears, sightings are rare in Florida. Even wildlife officials who work daily in the wilderness seldom see bears.

In Florida, there is little to fear from a bear encounter, although that knowledge might not stem the adrenaline flow. Unlike black bears elsewhere, Florida's subspecies is not known to attack humans. This does not mean caution should not be used around bears, particularly around females with young. Any wild animal should be left alone, and if encountered, treated cautiously.

Top: wild azalea along the Sante Fe River in O'Leno State Park.

Left: another view of the Sante Fe River at O'Leno.

Below: early morning along the Sante Fe River.

THE ORIGINS OF O'LENO

O'Leno was a lumbering town called Keno, after the gambling card game. When the people of the town found religion, and gambling was deemed sinful, the name was changed to Leno. As time went by, it was referred to as Old Leno, and has now come to us abbreviated as O'Leno.

OSCEOLA NATIONAL FOREST
(Baker and Columbia counties, 200,000 acres, multi-use)

The northern portions of this forest are truly rugged and impenetrable in places. There are four wild swampy areas: Big Gum, Buckhead and Pinhook swamps, and Impassable Bay.

Big Gum has two rugged trails, one of 2.5 and one of 5 miles, which do not connect. Miles and miles of forest roads are multi-use, as well as many of the trails. Trails for equestrian use total 50 miles. A 35-mile Florida Trail section trailhead is at Olustee, the site of Florida's most decisive Civil War battle. This section leads to the Suwannee River and the Stephen Foster Cultural Center in White Springs.

In addition to Ocean Pond, there are a few other smaller lakes, where deer are frequently seen. Osceola also has a sizable bear population in its forests and swamps. Major habitats: flatwoods, lakes, swamp, with some small rivers and streams.

Forest location. From I-75, exit east at Lake City on US-90, an east-west road that travels the length of the forest. Entrances into the forest are on the north side of US-90. With numerous forest roads, a forest map is the best way to explore. Maps can be obtained at the headquarters west of Olustee on US-90.

Top, left: a swamp with fall leaves on water.
Top, right: sunset at Ocean Pond.
Bottom: along a boardwalk over a cypress swamp on the Florida Trail in Osceola National Forest.

54

Top: alligator eyes illuminated by the flash of the camera.

Bottom, left: lotus along the lake shore at Paynes Prairie State Preserve.

Below: riders on an equestrian trail in Paynes Prairie State Preserve.

PAYNES PRAIRIE STATE PRESERVE
(Alachua County, 21,000+ acres, multi-use)

Among the famous naturalists who loved this prairie were William Bartram and Archie Carr. Bartram acknowledged the "savannah" in writings about his travels, while Dr. Carr wrote (from nearby University of Florida) of many wonders within the prairie, such as the horns of cattle covered with spider webs on a dewy morning.

Heavy rains in 1837 caused the water level of Alachua Lake to rise, flooding Paynes Prairie. The prairie is normally drained through the Alachua Sink. This sink became plugged, forming a lake so large it was able to carry steamboats. Then, suddenly, in 1891, the plug broke free, and the lake drained within a few days. Paynes Prairie is now a large basin marsh, wet most of the year, dry only for short periods, conditions which create a living bowl of flowers, grasses, and sedges.

Many trails within the preserve can be explored. While Paynes Prairie is multi-use, it is a good idea to check with rangers concerning which trails are available for which use. A portion of the Gainesville-Hawthorne State Trail, a "rail-to-trail," has its most scenic section here, although it is not on the old rail bed. There are also ranger-guided activities scheduled at various times.

Trails: Bolen Bluff, 3 miles. Chacala, 12 miles. Cones Dike, 8.25 miles. Gainesville-Hawthorne State Trail, 16 miles. Jackson's Gap Trail, 1.33 miles. La Chua, 2.5 miles. Lake, 1 mile. Wacahoota, 0.25 mile.

From I-75, exit south of Gainesville at Micanopy, go east to US-441, then north to the main entrance. Obtain a map at the entrance to locate the trails.

PELLICER CREEK CORRIDOR CONSERVATION AREA
(Flagler County, 3,865 acres, multi-use)

Pellicer Creek has marshes and flows into a saltwater estuary. There is also floodplain with hardwoods, and pine flatwoods with longleaf, and perhaps 5-6 miles of multi-use trail in intertwining loops. Primitive camping is available at designated sites. Botanists will appreciate cinnamon fern, orchids, and coontie. This conservation area is to the south of Faver-Dykes State Park, although you can't get there from here. Exit I-95 onto US-1 and Dixie Highway going south. From US-1, two miles south of Colfax, turn onto Old Kings Road and go east. *Managed by: St. Johns River Water Management District.*

RAINBOW SPRINGS STATE PARK
(Marion County, 600 acres, bicycling and hiking).

This former tourist attraction has man-made waterfalls, a first magnitude spring, and gardens for strolling. The official paved trail is 1.25 miles. Bicycle riding is on the paved entrance roads at the park and campground. The campground has considerable footpaths. There are service roads, and there are future plans to expand and develop trails. Located on the east side of US-41 north of Dunnellon, just south of SR-40.

Above and left: man-made waterfalls at Rainbow Springs State Park. Florida does have a number of naturally occurring, but rather short, waterfalls.

RALPH E. SIMMONS MEMORIAL STATE FOREST
(Nassau County, 3,688 acres, multi-use)

On one occasion there were large bear prints leading down the road some distance from the gate. Although bear tracks create great excitement, the bears are not always seen. Since this land borders Georgia, bear prints serve as a reminder that some of Florida's northern black bear population lives in both states.

The meandering St. Marys River serves as a boundary between Florida and Georgia. The river can be reached with 1 mile of hiking. Hardwoods and cypress along the winding, dark river provide splendid natural scenery.

All trails are multi-use on dirt roads, usually sufficiently firm for bicycles. Primitive camping is available at designated sites. There is plentiful sandhill with seemingly endless turkey oak. Within the area are several rare plants, including Bartram's ixia. Seepage and bog areas have pitcher plants. There also are orchids and toothache grass. Simmons is wild enough that bobcats and otters can sometimes be seen.

Just before US-301 leaves North Florida, turn east in Boulogne onto Lake Hampton Road and proceed a little over a mile to the first parking area. Or proceed farther to Penny Haddock Road and choose between two gates.

Managed by: St. Johns River Water Management District.

RICE CREEK SANCTUARY
(Putnam County, hiking)

This 3-mile loop through forest connects with the Florida Trail. Located six miles west of Palatka on SR-100. *Owned by: Georgia Pacific Paper Company.*

RIVER RISE STATE PRESERVE
(Columbia County, 4,000 acres, multi-use)

This is an extension of O'Leno State Park, and trails continue into it. The preserve encompasses a portion of the Sante Fe River, including some rapids, depending on water levels. This section receives heavy equestrian use. Use is through the management unit, O'Leno State Park. See O'Leno account for directions and use.

ROYAL TRAILS SEGMENT, FLORIDA TRAIL
(Lake County, hiking)

This 14.5-mile segment of the Florida Trail reaches from Cassia on SR-44 (the beginning of the Cassia segment) to Clearwater Lake in Ocala National Forest. Substantial sections are on road rights-of-way. *Managed by: Florida Trail Association.*

RUTH SPRINGS TRACT
(Suwannee County, 638 acres, multi-use)

The 6.5-mile trail, great for bicycling, includes 2.6 miles along the Suwannee River. The trail is mostly old road, very firm, with three loops, and two dead-ends at the river. The river is quite wide and fast-flowing here. Suwannee County maintains a small park in the center of the tract, where the spring bubbles or rages depending on water flow. The tract is part of the Troy Springs Conservation Area. Northwest of Branford, about 3 miles west of the Suwannee River, turn north from US-27 onto CR-425. There are well-placed signs. *Managed by: Suwannee River Water Management District.*

SAN FELASCO HAMMOCK STATE PRESERVE
(Alachua County, 6,900 acres, multi-use)

San Felasco is the most diverse hardwood hammock in Florida, with over 1500 plant species, 150 tree species, and 18 biological communities. The 10.4 miles of trail are revered by local joggers and were once used by an Olympic track team in training. Equestrian and bicycling trails have been built and are being expanded. In addition to the hammock, there are flatwoods and swamp, a small ravine area with two caves, and numerous white-tailed deer. Exit I-75 at SR-222 north of Gainesville. Go east 4 miles to NW 43d Street, and then north for 1 mile to SR-232 (Millhopper Road). Go west for 4 miles to the parking lot on the south side of the road.

SAWGRASS ISLAND PRESERVE
(Lake County, 1,137 acres, multi-use)

There are four trails: Bear Prairie, 2.6 miles; the North and South loops (1.35 miles each); and the Hammock Trail, 0.6 miles. All are connected. From the southern trailhead, the trail is not so easy to spot, as it lies across a field (rich in cactus) and begins in the oak treeline.

Although the area is multi-use, the sandy trail at this trailhead would make difficult bicycling. The northern trailhead is better suited for bicycling. There is adequate trailer parking at both trailheads.

One trick to finding it is to realize there is a SR-44 and a CR-44. Look for the county road. It is north of Eustis and south of Umatilla. It is crossed by SR-19. Turn west from SR-19 on CR-44. Turn northwest on CR-452. After 7 to 8 miles, turn east on Em-En-El Grove Road, and north on Thomas Boat Landing Road. After about 1 mile, turn east on Sawgrass Island Road. This becomes a path between homesteads until the path forks right and left. Left is the north trailhead. Right is the south trailhead.

Managed by: Lake County Water Authority.

STEINHATCHEE FALLS WILDLIFE MANAGEMENT AREA
(Dixie County, 7,046 acres, multi-use)

This is primarily pine plantations with hardwoods along the banks of the Steinhatchee River. The river runs through the western portion, where Steinhatchee Falls is found. It is a small waterfall in the north section just after the river bends south. It is difficult to imagine a waterfall, however slight, in this flat land along the Gulf Coast, but seeing is belieiving. Roads are multi-use, but due to sand, biking is difficult. Approximately half of the acres above are on private land open only for hunting during season. Located 27 miles south of Perry, along and west of US-19. It is also bordered by CR-358 and CR-51. *Managed by: Florida Fish and Wildlife Conservation Commission.*

Top: a limestone outcrop in San Felasco Hammock State Preserve.

Above: two young men cool off on a hot day at Ruth Springs, a summertime tradition in North Florida.

STEPHEN FOSTER STATE FOLK CULTURE CENTER
(Columbia County, bicycling and hiking)

Many come here for the museum and carillon tower. There are also 10 miles of bicycle or hiking trails. The Center is the southeast terminus of the Suwannee River Segment of the Florida Trail, a 51.4-mile section extending west to the Withlacoochee River Bridge on SR-141. It is also the trailhead for the 35-mile Osceola National Forest segment. From I-75, take the White Springs exit east, and follow the prominent signs.

STOKES LANDING CONSERVATION AREA
(St. Johns County, 274 acres, multi-use)

This small area is along the Tolamato River, which separates it from Guana River State Park. A marsh lies between the uplands and the river. The trail is 3 miles long. From US-1, north of the St. Augustine Regional Airport, take Venetian Boulevard a short distance east, then turn south on Old Dixie Road, and east again on Lakeshore Drive. *Managed by: St. Johns River Water Management District.*

SUNNYHILL RESTORATION AREA
(Marion County, 4,357 acres, multi-use)

This land (along the Ocklawaha River and adjoining Ocala National Forest) was purchased to restore the wetlands and a portion of the historic river. It is the sort of waterway where a family can be found fishing with cane poles on an idyllic day, and the only disturbance is the occasional roaring powerboat setting the banks awash in its wake. A multi-use trail on the levee is 6.5 miles between Sunnyhill and Moss Bluff. A return multi-use trail passes along the Ocala National Forest boundary, and on FR-8. Vehicles could be parked at both locations, or the trip could be made as a loop. The total distance would likely be between 13 and 14 miles. Primitive camping is available at designated sites.

The entrance is 5.9 miles east of Weirsdale, just east of the Ocklawaha River on the north side of SR-42 and a little hard to spot. Another entrance at Moss Bluff Recreation Area is north of Lake Weir on CR-464 before the junction with CR-314A. *Managed by: St. Johns River Water Management District*

SUWANNEE RIVER GREENWAY BRANFORD
See Branford Rail-to-Trail

SUWANNEE SPRINGS, LINVILLE TRACT
(Suwannee County, 308 acres, multi-use)

Approximately 10 miles of trail lie along the Suwannee within these two adjoining tracts of the Woods Ferry Conservation Area. Two miles are along the river banks. The equestrian ride is simply terrific.

Sulfur water from Suwannee Springs was once believed to have healing powers (some still think it does). The remnants of an old, stone bath house are beside the river. It was a busy place where tourists with ailments sought relief in the early part of the 20th Century.

Across the street is the Spirit of the Suwannee Music Park. Camping and stabling are available. The address and phone number are in the Appendix.

From I-75, south of Jasper, exit south on US-129. Or from I-10, near Live Oak, exit north on US-129. Proceed 5 miles in either case to Suwannee Springs on the east side of US-129. *Managed by: Suwannee River Water Management District.*

Top and bottom: **the Suwannee River as seen from Suwannee Springs.**

SUWANNEE RIVER STATE PARK
(Madison and Suwannee counties, 1,800 acres, bicycling and hiking)

There are not enough adjectives to do justice to this park. It becomes a favorite for many visitors because of its varied beauty. It very well could be the most beautiful park in Florida.

It is located at the confluence of the (northern) Withlacoochee and Suwannee rivers, and during high water, powerful jets cascade into both rivers from spring runs. These rivers are fast-flowing, often at 4 miles an hour, faster than a fast hiker.

Every trail in or around this park offers exceptional views. You will surely want to visit this area many times in different seasons. The Ellaville rapids are to the northwest outside the park, and the incredible Lime Sink Run is within the park to the east.

This park is the start of the Ellaville segment of the Florida Trail and the end of the Suwannee segment. Bicycling is allowed on the paved road, but the main reason to come here is for the splendid hiking and scenery.

Trails: Big Oak, Florida Trail Loop, 11.2 miles. Ellaville Section, Florida Trail, 18 miles. Lime Sink Run, 7 miles. Nature Trails, 3 miles. Suwannee River Section, Florida Trail, 47 miles.

Located off I-10 or US-90. Prominent signs on both highways lead to the park, 6 miles northwest of Live Oak.

Top, left: a small spring feeds into the Withlacoochee River (North).

Top, right: Lime Sink takes its name from the adjacent limestone outcroppings.

Below: the seeds of hearts-a-bursting.

Bottom right: the Alapaha Rise, where the river flows out of the ground to join the Suwanne River.

TALBOT GEOPARK
(Duval County, 8,000+ acres, multi-use)

The GeoPark includes five island units: Amelia Island State Recreation Area, three state parks (Big and Little Talbot, and Ft. George), and Long Island. There are steep cliffs, at least by Florida standards, beaches with hardwoods along the dunes, tidal flats, and saltmarsh.

Amelia Island has horse rentals for a thundering ride along the beach. There are miles of shore to be walked on the five units, and more than 10 miles of bicycling and hiking trails. A special bicycle path on Ft. George Island follows the fairways of an abandoned golf course. This is located on the road to the Kingsley Plantation. All these are located along A1A, north of Jacksonville. There are prominent signs.

Bicyling: Ft. George, 4.4 mile road, 2.5-mile trail. **Equestrian:** Amelia Island, 5 mile, horse rentals. **Hiking:** Amelia Island, 1.5 mile beach. Big Talbot, 5-mile trail. Ft. George 2.5-mile trail. Little Talbot, 5-mile trail plus 5 miles of beach.

The two major units in the GeoPark are Big and Little Talbot Island state parks. At Big Talbot, in particular, the emphasis is on keeping the 1,000 acres in a natural state. Little Talbot is a larger park with 2,500 acres, and has RV and tent camping.

Top: algae-covered limestone and driftwood along the beach at Big Talbot Island.

Below: Indian pipes are found in the woods and scrub in Central, North, and Northwest Florida.

THE KINGSLEY PLANTATION

Run by the National Park Service, Kingsley Plantation is located on Ft. George Island. Kingsley was a businessman engaged in many ventures before Florida was part of the US. He was a white slave holder who married an African woman. When Florida became part of the US, Kingsley moved his family to Haiti because of what he felt was an unbearable climate of prejudice and hatred. Kingsley Plantation offers a glimpse back in time to see what life on a plantation was like, as well as giving a glimpse into the lives of Kingsley and his wife.

TIGER BAY STATE FOREST
(Volusia County, 23,425 acres, multi-use)

This forest is between Daytona Beach and Deland. Located to the west of the Tomoka River, and to the south of the Little Tomoka River, the primary habitats are swamp and pine forest, with two small lakes. It is a nesting place for eagles and a corridor for species such as bear. While numerous roads are open for multi-use, a 12-mile designated equestrian trail and a nature trail have been created on the north side of US-92. There are three entrances along US-92, west of I-95. A northern entrance is located on Lima Ridge/Tomoka Road off of SR-40, just west of I-95.

Managed by: Division of Forestry and St. Johns River Water Management District.

WALDO RAIL-TO-TRAIL
(Alachua County, bicycling and hiking)

This is a little less than 6-miles round trip, on a paved path on a former CSX bed in Gainesville. The trailhead is on SR-222 and Northeast 39th Avenue near Waldo Road. The Depot Trail intersects the Waldo Trail and travels for 2 miles from the Shands Hospital to the intersection with SR-26. *Managed by: City of Gainesville.*

WELAKA STATE FOREST
(Putnam County, 2,288 acres, multi-use)

To the north of Lake George, and to the east of the St. Johns River, Welaka is located in some impressive natural country. It has gorgeous floodplain along the St. Johns, with cypress, maple, and tupelo. Among its other habitats are flatwoods, hammock, marsh, ponds, and sandhill.

The forest brochure does not mention bicycling, possibly because of the emphasis on equestrian use. There is a 72-stall stable available, and a 6.5-mile loop through the sandhills and longleaf pine.

There are two hiking trails. The Mud Spring Trail is 2 miles long. Mud Spring flows into Lake George. The St. Johns Landing Trail is 4.5 miles, partially on old railroad bed.

The forest is east of CR-309, south of Welaka. From US-17 in Crescent City, turn west on CR-308, then go north on CR-309.
Managed by: Division of Forestry.

WHITE SPRINGS TRACT
(Hamilton County, 269 acres)

There are two bicycle and hiking trails of 4 and 5 miles each on the southeast banks of the Suwannee River in White Springs. The shorter trail is known as White Springs Trail, and the longer one Bridge-to-Bridge Trail. There are some interesting challenges for bicyclists. The trails are also open to hiking. From US-41 in the south of White Springs, go west on Adams Memorial Drive. The trailhead is across the street from the cemetery. *Managed by: Suwannee River Water Management District.*

Top: the Ellaville area of the Suwannee River along the Florida Trail. Unless the water level is high, there are rapids in this section.
Bottom: limestone outcrops along the Withlacoochee River (North).

TWIN RIVERS STATE FOREST
(Hamilton, Madison, and Suwannee counties, 14,774 acres, multi-use)

The twin rivers are the Suwannee and the northern Withlacoochee, two of the most breathtaking rivers in Florida, with many wonderful vistas. One of the highlights on the Suwannee is the Ellaville portion of the Florida Trail, which passes a short run of whitewater rapids.

This forest includes separated tracts beginning in the south at Mill Creek and ending in the north along CR-150. The tracts are: Anderson Springs, Black, Blue Springs, Chitty Bend, Ellaville, Longleaf, Mill Creek North and South, Nekoosa, Sullivan, Westwood, and Withlacoochee. Ellaville is the largest tract at 4,250 acres.

A brochure and map from Division of Forestry helps to show the way.

Equestrian use is allowed in the forest's Black, Blue Springs, Ellaville, Mill Creek, Sullivan, and Westwood tracts. There is bicycling in Anderson, Black, Ellaville, Mill Creek South, Withlacoochee, and Westwood. Hiking opportunities are in all units except Nekoosa, and the bicycle and horse trails are open to hikers. An 18-mile portion of the Florida Trail runs through Twin Rivers from Suwannee River State Park, by the Ellaville Rapids, toward the other terminus in Branford. Trailwalker Trails are in the Ellaville and Anderson tracts.

The Ellaville section is along US-90 to the west of Suwannee River State Park.
Managed by: Division of Forestry.

THE SUWANNEE BICYCLE ASSOCIATION

Many of the trails on Suwannee River Water Management Lands, called Conservation Areas, have been created or maintained by the Suwannee Bicycle Association. The association has an office in White Springs, open mostly on weekends. Contact information is in the Appendix. This fine organization deserves a special thanks from naturalists and recreational users of these trails. As with the Florida Trail Association, the work is voluntary, and funding by private donations.

DEVIL'S MILLHOPPER STATE GEOLOGICAL SITE
(Alachua County)

The short nature trail around a 15,000 year old sinkhole will not leave you winded. But hiking back up the boardwalk from the bottom of the sinkhole might. The sinkhole is full of lush vegetation, including ferns and trees, and ground water often pours out of fissures in the walls. The Millhopper is such a marvel that many locals visit it daily. The sinkhole is perhaps 150 deep and 450 feet across. Located on SR-232 (Millhopper Road) in northwest Gainesville (see directions to San Felasco Hammock).

FAVER-DYKES STATE PARK
(St. Johns County)

A designated canoe trail, Pellicer Creek, flows by the park. For the hiker, there are two short nature trails and usually plentiful wildlife. From the junction of I-95 and US-1, proceed north less than 0.5 miles, and turn east at the prominent sign.

LITTLE SHOALS TRACT
(Columbia County, 267 acres)

A 2.5-mile, multi-use trail begins at a small white water rapids on the Suwannee River. Enter on US-41, 1 mile south of White Springs, near the inspection station (on east side of the road).

RAVINE STATE GARDENS
(Putnam County)

In 1933, the Federal Works Project planted a garden in this natural ravine. The ravine itself was originally created by water flowing beneath the sand ridges on the St. Johns River shoreline. A 1.8-mile paved trail around the ravine is beloved by local joggers and walkers. There are many foot trails up and down the ravine and through the garden. An azalea festival is held in March and April when the gardens are in full bloom. Located in Palatka on Twigg Street.

Top, right: Crystal Lake Ravine along a Florida Trail segment.
Middle, left: spectacular rock outcrops on the beach side of Washington Oaks State Gardens.
Bottom: the waterfall at Falling Creek, south of White Springs.

SILVER RIVER STATE PARK
(Marion County)

One short trail takes hikers to the banks of this attractive river flowing from Silver Springs (scenic in many ways, as it has appeared in several motion pictures). A longer loop trail passes by a large sinkhole, sandhill, and through flatwoods. From SR-40 in Silver Springs, go south on CR-35 to the entrance.

TOMOKA STATE PARK
(Volusia County)

A short nature trail takes the visitor to the outdoor statue created by Fred Dana depicting the "Legend of Tomokie." There is also a museum dedicated to Dana's art. Bicycling is allowed on the roads, and there are bike rentals. On Beach Street in Ormond Beach.

WASHINGTON OAKS
STATE GARDENS
(Flagler County)

On the beachside of A1A, is a 2-mile round trip along coastal scrub, highlighted by a large outcrop of 100,000 year old coquina limestone. Along the river, 1.6 miles of hiking and biking are possible on the Timucuan and Jungle Road trails combined. There is also a short nature trail and a stroll through the gardens. Located along A1A, 2 miles south of Marineland.

Top and bottom: **trails in Ravine State Garden in Palatka.**

MB-SI

While Central Florida has great diversity, it is a region of prominent scrub habitat, some of the most precious still surviving on the Central or Lake Wales Ridge. Although as much as 70% of scrub has been lost to human use, a large area remains, and its value is now established for preservation. If you hike, bike, or gallop along trails in Central Florida, you will come upon scrub. It is easy to recognize.

Scrub is typified by several signature plants and trees, among them Florida rosemary and sand pine, both common within the region. The bird most closely associated with scrub, the Florida scrub-jay, is threatened because it only nests in this diminished habitat. Probably the most diverse representation of scrub, including a great variety of scrub plants, is found in Lake Wales Ridge State Forest, particularly in the Lake Arbuckle Tract.

An historically large area of Central Florida is the Green Swamp, the headwaters of the Hillsborough, Peace, and Withlacoochee rivers. This area falls within the Southwest Florida Water Management District. In addition to many outstanding state and county parks, preserves, and recreation areas, many recreational

Top: **a great egret hunting below cypress in the shallows of Weeki Wachee River.**

opportunities are available on district lands, some newly opened to the public.

Central and South Florida have the disadvantage for bicyclists and hikers of being exceptionally hot, routinely reaching 90 degrees during the late spring and summer seasons. The heat factor also applies to all recreational activities in South Florida almost all year long. Many choose to bicycle or hike in these two regions early in the day.

ALDERMAN-FORD PARK
(Hillsborough County, 1,140 acres, bicycling and hiking)

This is a wonderful place where a gopher tortoise might lumber through the picnic area, fence lizards might sprint across the path, and marsh rabbits can make sudden skittish appearances. Many families use this area, particularly on weekends.

From the picnic area at the main entrance, there is a paved trail of 1.8 miles, complete with exercise stations, and an unpaved loop trail of probably 3 miles, used by both bicyclists and hikers. The paved trail has boardwalks crossing the Alafia River which are remarkable constructions for a small county park.

A bit south of the main entrance, is a turn-off to a canoe launch on the Alafia River. Instead of going to the launch, follow the road. It leads to more miles of hiking through openings in three places through the fence line. This is mostly a shaded park with hardwood floodplain, mixed forest, some pine flatwoods, and river.

From I-4, take the SR-39 exit south a considerable distance from Plant City. Or from SR-60, take SR-39 north.

Managed by: Hillsborough County.

AVON PARK BOMBING RANGE
(Polk County, 106,000 acres, equestrian and hiking)

Avon Park Bombing Range is located on "Bombing Range Ridge," 7 miles from the Lake Wales Ridge.

There are two Lake Arbuckle Trails in the Florida Trail system, this one, and the other in Lake Wales Ridge State Forest. The 16-mile trail in Avon Park, used by hikers and horse riders, starts in scrub, then changes quickly between floodplain, scrub, and flatwoods. This long trail is surpassed by the 27-mile Lake Kissimmee portion of the Florida Trail, also passing through a portion of the military base.

The 6-mile Sandy Point Wildlife Refuge is a little-used loop. It is a convoluted series of mowed walks, including one through the flatwoods, past a hammock, and into a prairie where a cattle herd grazes.

The overlook from the 0.5-mile boardwalk of the Lake Arbuckle Nature Trail seems too good to be true and should not be missed. The lake edge is filled with lush ferns, hardwoods, and at least four types of air plants (epiphytes). On the lake shore are birds, snakes, and exceptional tranquillity. In the lake, pond lilies bloom spectacularly in season.

There are unfortunately things to scare away potential hikers. The bombing ranges have unexploded munitions and dangerous phosphorous flares. There is a state prison on the installation, and there is a juvenile work center as well. Like most things we are afraid of, reason will hopefully win out over fear, despite the long, "hold harmless" agreement the installation requires "recreationists" to sign. The bombing ranges are not on the trails, and while munitions might be found, they are not plentiful because they are usually dropped on the bombing range. The criminals are locked up, and crime is not a contagious disease.

Once you accept this, then gaining access could still be a problem. The base closes to the public Monday and opens Thursday night. However, if there is weekend bombing, portions are closed to "recreationists." It is not often that the whole base is closed, but partial closings are fairly frequent.

From Avon Park, the base is east at the end of CR-64 and adjacent to Lake Wales Ridge State Forest. Call on Thursday mornings to find out if the installation is open to the public over the weekends, and if portions are closed. The phone number is in the Appendix.

Above: a hiker stops to examine an area covered with deer moss, a lichen which is found in many scrub habitats.

THE ALAFIA RIVER CORRIDOR

Alderman-Ford is located along the south prong of the Alafia River. The lands along the south and north prong together make up the "corridor," sensitive lands purchased or in the process of public acquisition.

The Alafia is a scenic, twisting, blackwater river that receives a good deal of recreational use. Jet skis, canoes, kayaks, and fishing boats abound. However, the river is sick. The land acquisition process has nothing to do with the tragic events of 1998, when a phosphoric acid plume from a phosphate company traveled 37 miles down river, killing probably over a million fish and shellfish (the phosphate company claims a lower number). Portions of the river remain a "dead zone." Both residents and environmentalists are concerned that little has been done to make up for the damage. The phosphate company admits responsibility, but may lack the funds for a clean-up.

The Alafia Banks are two spoil islands at the mouth of the river that serve as nesting grounds for thousands of birds. Sixteen species have rookeries there, including herons, ibis, pelicans, and spoonbills.

BALM BOYETTE SCRUB PRESERVE
(Hillsborough County, 5,000 acres, bicycling and hiking)

Balm Boyette is popular with bicyclists, is known for its physical challenges, and also for its opportunities for nature observation. There is a two-lane, sandy, 10-mile road with little shade, and a single lane, 9-mile hewn path. The path twists and winds through sand pine scrub. Florida golden aster is found at Balm Boyette. This is a rare endemic plant found only in Hillsborough County scrub.

From I-75, exit on CR-672 and go east 1.5 miles to US-301. Go south about 1 mile on US-301 and turn east again on CR-672. A little more than 5 miles later, turn north on Balm Boyette Road and proceed to the obvious trailhead on the east side of the road.

Managed by: Hillsborough County.

BLUE CYPRESS CONSERVATION AREA
(Indian River County, 52,671 acres, bicycling and hiking)

Blue Cypress Lake allegedly takes its name from the bluish reflection of its waters onto the trunks of its many cypress trees. The lake is roughly 21 square miles: 3 miles wide, 7 miles long. It is considered by many to be the most beautiful of the Central Florida lakes. The area is floodplain, lake, marsh, river basin, and swamp associated with the St. Johns River.

In the early 20th Century, a levee and road separated Blue Cypress Lake from the St. Johns and its headwater marshes. The area was developed for agriculture, and the river was turned into a channel. As with the Everglades, there was a tremendous decline in winter bird populations, and sawgrass was replaced by cordgrass.

The trail is essentially along grassy dikes, perhaps 8 miles long. It is accessed through the Blue Cypress Recreation Area on CR-512. It can be used for hiking or bicycling, but there is no equestrian use.

The lake itself can barely be observed from the overlook at the end of Blue Cypress Lake Road. The lake is exceptionally beautiful and deserving of a boat ride. Look for otters. They are even seen running along the road, for reasons known only to otters.

From I-95, exit on CR-512 through Fellsmere for the recreation area. The county road leads to the conservation area and trails. SR-60 also borders the south end for observing the lake or canoeing it, but there are no trails there. The SR-60 entrance (Blue Cypress Road) is 5 miles east of Yeehaw Junction and the Florida Turnpike.

Managed by: St. Johns River Water Management District.

BLUE SPRING STATE PARK
(Volusia County, 3,200 acres, multi-use)

This spring (one of Florida's 27 first magnitude springs) flows into the St. Johns River. It was visited by the famous naturalist, William Bartram.

It is absolutely the best place in Florida to see large numbers of manatees on cold mornings. A boardwalk has been built along the spring run, and at times 60 or more manatees take shelter in the comparatively warmer waters. The manatee is the "mermaid" that came in from the cold. The constant temperature of spring water offers a life-saving reprieve during cold winter months. The name, manatee, reportedly comes from the West Indian word for breast, *manati*. As mammals, they do nurse their young, although the mother's nipples are underneath the flippers.

Calling Blue Spring multi-use is stretching it, yet it is. There is an equestrian trail of 1 mile, essentially a dirt path. Bicycling is confined to the paved roads, which are usually pretty busy. A 4-mile hiking trail must be hiked in then out, for a total of 8 miles, and passes through flatwoods, hammock, marsh, and scrub. Aside from the manatees, this hiking trail is the star feature of the park. This is a busy park, particularly in winter, and there is a large campground.

From I-4, exit on US-17/92. There are many US-17/92 signs on I-4, but the park is announced prominently by a sign on I-4 near Orange City. In Orange City, turn west onto French Avenue, and follow the signs to the park.

Top: **the lakeshore with water lilies at Blue Cypress Conservation Area. This is a breathtakingly beautiful lake with attractive cypress. It is popular for birding and fishing, and has many otters.**

BOYD HILL NATURE PARK
(Pinellas County, 245 acres, bicycling and hiking)

Boyd Hill is to be celebrated, not just for the recreational use it offers to so many, or for the views of Lake Maggiore, or even for the amount of volunteer work that has gone into it. It should be revered for its very existence.

Boyd Hill preserves some flatwoods, hammock, marsh, and scrub in the midst of suburbia. Thanks to it, local school children and budding naturalists have a place to go. It is now one of the few locations in Pinellas County where such commonplace Florida sights as an alligator or a sand pine can still be seen. Boyd Hill is, in fact, a singular island of nature in a sea of golf courses, schools, churches, residences, businesses, sports domes, and clogged highways.

It has 3.5 miles of paved trail and boardwalk for bicycles and foot travel, and is loved by local joggers.

Also, it is exceptionally hard to find. Take the 54th Avenue South exit from I-275 in St. Petersburg. Go east for 2 miles to the light at 9th Street South (Martin Luther King Street). Turn north to Country Club Way South. Turn west onto Country Club. The park is beside the library.

Managed by: Pinellas County.

BUCK LAKE CONSERVATION AREA
(Volusia County, 9,291 acres, multi-use)

Buck Lake Conservation Area is north of Seminole Ranch Conservation Area on the north side of SR-46. Approximately one-third of the property is swamp near the St. Johns River, and the remainder is a mix of flatwoods, hammock with palm and oak, marsh, and scrub. Two small lakes are on the property, and several creeks. Scrub-jays are found within the conservation area.

The multi-use trails along Morgan Alderman Road are either along the power line, or on a mowed road. Two parking areas along SR-46 are clearly identified with water management district signs, necessary since there are a number of dwellings along the road which could be mistaken for entry points. The multi-use trail there is probably 8 miles in length. There are four designated primitive campsites, including one on the lake.

Located approximately 10 miles east of Oviedo on SR-46 on the eastern bank of the St. Johns. Morgan Alderman Road is the first road on the north on the east bank of the St. Johns. The two parking lots along SR-46 are a few miles farther.

Managed by: St. Johns River Water Management District.

BULL CREEK WILDLIFE MANAGEMENT AREA
(Osceola County, 23,504 acres, multi-use)

Although popular with local hunters, this is a remote location, wild and primitive, and its multi-use trails are little-used. Habitats include: flatwoods, hardwood hammock, marsh, scrub, and swamp. There is a small population of red-cockaded woodpeckers in the large pines.

In addition to 8.6 miles of multi-use roads,

there is a 17-mile section of the Florida Trail. Primitive camping is permitted. The Florida Trail enters and exits on lands belonging to Deseret Ranch, a very large, scenic, Mormon-owned enterprise. Three Lakes Wildlife Management Area is west of Bull Creek. Access is limited during hunts in all three areas.

Levee L-73 is a popular trail with bicyclists and hikers. It is identified on the recreational guide of the water management district and on the map on the back of the hunting regulations for Bull Creek.

Located 28 miles to the west of Melbourne, equidistant from I-95 and US-441, Bull Creek can be reached by going west from I-95, and taking US-192 west to Crabgrass Road on the south side of the road. There is a prominent sign. It is 5 miles on graded road to the check station and entrance.

Managed by: St. Johns River Water Management District.

Top: a swimmer enjoys the water at Blue Spring State Park. The spring run is very active with manatees, large catfish, gar, and mullet.

CADY WAY TRAIL
(Orange County, bicycling and hiking)

This rail-to-trail is 3.6 miles in one direction through suburbia, alongside residences and the Orlando Fashion Square Mall. It is paved and open for bicyclists, hikers, joggers, and skaters. It is heavily used, and has bike racks, shelter, and water. From Colonial Drive, the southern trailhead is reached by going north on Maguire Boulevard and then south on Bennet Road. The northern trailhead in Orlando is reached by taking CR-436 to Cady Way. Colonial Drive is SR-50 and it intersects CR-436 to the east of the mall. *Managed by: Orange County.*

CALADESI ISLAND STATE PARK
(Pinellas County, 1,650 acres, hiking)

Perhaps 5 miles of untouched beaches can be walked. Caladesi is an excellent place to see schools of dolphin, and sea turtles nest on the island. A nature trail behind the dunes is approximately 4 miles in length. Caladesi can be reached by ferry from nearby Honeymoon Island. From north of Dunedin on Alternate US-19, go west at SR-586.

CANAVERAL MARSHES CONSERVATION AREA
(Brevard County, 9,545 acres, multi-use)

East of the Tosohatchee State Reserve, the conservation area parallels 20-25 miles of river shoreline, and is mostly floodplain and marsh of the St. Johns. It is also located south of Seminole Ranch Conservation Area, but access to that area is not very good from SR-50. Perhaps 3 miles in, 3 miles out, the multi-use trails are essentially on water management roads. The Florida Trail is accessed from the Great Outdoors Resort. From I-95, near Indian River City, go west on SR-50 to the parking area on the south side of the road just east of the river. *Managed by: St. Johns River Water Management District.*

CANAVERAL NATIONAL SEASHORE
(Brevard and Volusia counties, 59,300 acres, bicycling and hiking)

Vapor trails in the early morning are a routine sight across most of Central Florida. While space travel might not yet have caught up to the movies, it has become commonplace enough that launches, even spectacular ones at night, attract little interest. It is more likely that the landing, which rattles windows, will serve as a reminder a shuttle is returning. Taking space travel for granted, it is easy to forget that the rockets are potentially explosive fuel and hunks of metal. The buffer zone, in case of accident, includes both Canaveral National Seashore and Merritt Island National Wildlife Refuge.

While there are several short hiking trails, visitors come mostly for the more than 20 miles of continuous pristine beach. This is the longest stretch of natural beach remaining on the eastern coast of Florida. The beach and the wildlife refuge are often closed during launch windows. Bicycles can be ridden on the paved roads, but these are quite busy on winter weekends.

Canaveral National Seashore, especially the Volusia portion, is currently popular with naturists. Visitors there might encounter nude sunbathers.

Take the Titusville exit east from I-95 and go through the city. Cross the Indian River on CR-406 and follow the signs.

CARLTON TRACT.
See Gum Slough

CARTER ROAD PARK
(Polk County, 400+ acres, multi-use)

Behind the soccer fields at this recreational complex are 5-6 miles of multi-use hard-packed roads around former phosphate pits, which have become fishing lakes.

Around the pits, and over the artificial mounds, a bicycle trail winds perilously close to the edge. It is a favorite "technical" ride for many. Ardent bicyclists have a number of interesting phrases such as "endo," for flipping end-over-end. "Technical" means there are a lot of obstacles, and there is a good chance of doing an "endo" on this trail if you ride it like a "kamikaze." This trail is a real workout because of the climbs and obstacles.

From I-4, take the Polk East-West Tollroad to Florida Avenue (SR-37) and go south. Carter Road is the first road on the left after Shepherd Road, perhaps 5 miles from the Tollroad.

CATFISH CREEK STATE PRESERVE
(Polk County, 5,000 acres, multi-use)

The preserve has also been called the Broussard Preserve. Within this scrub preserve, are 9 miles of service roads and a 6-mile hiking trail on the Lake Wales Ridge. Although designated multi-use, the sand is very deep, and bicycling is beyond challenging. There is cutthroat grass in the seeps, pine flatwoods, and Lake Hatchineha. East of Lake Hamilton, from SR-17, turn east on CR-542. This is Lake Hamilton Road, and it becomes Lake Hatchineha Road. Before reaching the popular fishing lake, turn south onto Firetower Road. The trailhead is on the east side of the road within 2 to 3 miles. *Managed by: Lake Kissimmee State Park.*

CHASSAHOWITZKA WILDLIFE MANAGEMENT AREA
(Hernando County, 29,000+ acres, hiking)

This is one of six wildlife management areas where new recreational trails are scheduled to be constructed. Here they will be built on an abandoned railroad tram that leads to one of the oldest hardwood swamps south of the Suwannee. Their completion, according to the Florida Fish and Wildlife Conservation Commission, is imminent, and will result in 15 to 25 miles of trails, perhaps with optional overnight camping by permit. One entrance is from US-19, 8 miles north of Weeki Wachee. The other entrance consists of deep sand roads requiring a four-wheel drive. There the predominant habitat is sand pine scrub. A trailhead is planned for each entrance. The sandy entrance can be reached from US-19 by going west on CR-550. *Managed by: Florida Fish and Wildlife Conservation Commission.*

CHULUOTA WILDERNESS AREA
(Seminole County, 625 acres, multi-use)

There are two multi-use loop trails: the East Loop is 2.6 miles, while the West Loop is 2.7. They pass through flatwoods, hammock, marsh, scrub, and swamp. The area is east of Chuluota in the southeast corner of the county. From Chuluota, take CR-419 to Curreyville Road. Take the sharp right and stay on Curreyville Road after it meets Mills Lake Road. The entrance is on the south side after a few additional miles. *Managed by: Seminole County.*

CROSS SEMINOLE TRAIL
(Seminole County, bicycling and hiking)

The Lake Jessup segment of the Florida Trail passes through on an old railroad bed. This is a favorite bicycle trip, 3.5 miles each way. There are plans to expand this rail-to-trail into nearby Winter Springs, with an estimated completed length of 14 miles. Located northwest of Oviedo at the junction of CR-434 and SR-426. *Managed by: Seminole County.*

CYPRESS CREEK WELLFIELD
(Pasco County, 74,000 acres, multi-use)

Cypress Creek is a tributary of the Hillsborough River. From the parking site in the Wellfield, a road passes by flatwoods, floodplain, hardwood swamp, and swamp dominated by cypress. The woods are dense, and deer and hawks are easily seen.

There are four trails: two hiking, one bicycle, and one equestrian. The trails are approximately 1 to 2 miles each, but connected to the road. The journey is 3 to 4 miles in and out, if using one trail, more if using several trails. Check before using the equestrian trail as it is sometimes closed.

From I-75, go west on CR-54 to US-41. Go north on US-41, then turn northeast on CR-583 and follow the signs to Cypress Creek Wellfield on CR-582 (Ehren Cutoff). Watch the signs closely as it is easy to miss the turnoff.

Managed by: Southwest Florida Water Management District.

Opposite page: a scene along the Hillsborough River in Hillsborough River State Park.

DEAD RIVER SITE
(Hillsborough County, 21 acres, bicycling and hiking)

This is part of the larger Lower Hillsborough Flood Detention Area (Wilderness Park), which includes more than 17,000 acres. The road leading into the site is paved or shell, 2 miles each way. It is a favorite bicycle ride, in part because the hardwood floodplain provides so much shade. It is a journey under canopy, and which is also enjoyed by hikers and joggers. One reward is a glimpse of the Hillsborough River from an old bridge.

Formerly, the only trail here was the one trampled down by fishermen and wildlife along the river bank. However, a wide, mowed path has been created that connects to Hillsborough River State Park. This trail is 2 miles each way, and the entrance into the state park is little known. The trailhead is at the parking lot at the end of the paved road. Deer are frequently seen in the shadows beneath the trees in the floodplain.

Exit from I-4 onto US-301 north. This site is 1 mile south of Hillsborough River State Park on the west side of the road. The road is closed to vehicles Monday through Thursday. *Managed by: Southwest Florida Water Management District.*

(THE NATURE CONSERVANCY'S) DISNEY WILDERNESS PRESERVE
(Orange County, 12,000 acres, hiking)

This land was a set-aside resulting from Disney's development around Orlando. It was given to the Nature Conservancy. They have used the land for education and research.

There is a 4.5-mile hiking loop, with a shorter 2.5-mile option. In addition to pine flatwoods, a little scrub, and a cypress swamp, there is Lake Russell, where sometimes otters are seen at the overlook. There is also a 0.5-mile, self-guided, interpretative trail.

A chalkboard at the trailhead encourages visitors to write down what they saw that day. One young visitor, either very lucky, or possibly having an overactive imagination, wrote: "Bobcat, otter, pygmy rattlesnake, deer, armadillo, cottonmouth, osprey." Even one such sighting would be a joy for most.

From Kissimmee, go west on US17-92, then south 8 miles on CR-531.

DUETTE PARK
(Manatee County, 22,000 acres, multi-use)

This is a water conservation area with the trails on 8 miles of multi-use roads. There is mostly new growth and little shade. Sun block and water are in order. From I-75, take 301 to SR-62 in Parrish, then east 19 miles to Duette Road (this is approximately 26 miles from I-75). *Managed by: Manatee County.*

ECON RIVER WILDERNESS AREA
(Seminole County, 230 acres, equestrian and hiking)

There is a 3-mile hiking trail, and the land is open for horseback riding. The area sits on

Top: the beautiful canopy road leading into Dead River Site. It is named Dead River because it does not have its own water source. Rather, at times of high water, the Hillsborough River flows into it.

the county line with Orange County. It is south of the city of Oviedo, on the west bank of the Econlockhatchee River. Take SR-434 (Alafaya Trail) to McColloch Road and turn east, then turn north on Lockwood Road which leads into the entrance. *Managed by: Seminole County.*

FLAGLER TRAIL
(Seminole County, bicycling and hiking)

This is an un-paved path on a former railroad bed. It passes through or by a number of public lands owned by the state and county. It is also called the Old State Road 13 Trail. A parking area has been established on Lake Lenelle Drive. This is reached from CR-419 southeast of Oviedo by turning north on Langford Drive. The trail goes east for 3.25 miles then is broken, and resumes on SR-46 by a fire station to continue another 3.5 miles. The only trailhead at present, however, is at Lake Lennelle Drive. There are ambitious plans to acquire property to connect and expand this trail. Future editions of this book will include updates. *Managed by: Seminole County.*

FLATWOODS PARK
(Hillsborough County, 3,700 acres, bicycling and hiking)

Flatwoods includes 7 miles of paved loop designated one direction only, for bicyclists, hikers, and roller bladers. This is a completely open trail, but ice water coolers are available at four locations along the way.

Off-road trails and exits to nearby access points provide additional distance. Parking at the Visitor's Center and pedaling to the trailhead can also increase the round trip to close to 9 miles. Parking on Bruce B. Downs and traveling to the loop is 2 miles in, 2 miles out.

Special events include moonlight rides in cooler months. This is an exceptionally popular bicycling area on weekends, often drawing 600 or more riders a day.

Besides pine and oak dominated palmetto flatwoods, there are some substantial cypress swamps and small marshes along the trail. Slash pine was timbered out in May and June of 2000, and the open areas created are expected to blossom with growth. Amazingly, a Florida panther seems to have spent enough time in Flatwoods to have been frequently seen just prior to the lumbering.

Wildlife spotting is unpredictable in Flatwoods. Some weeks there is nothing moving except the sweat down the foreheads of hikers. Yet other days the flatwoods are filled with wildlife, including deer which generally sit passively as bicyclists breeze by.

From I-75 in Tampa, go east on Fletcher Avenue which becomes Morris Bridge Road. Seven miles from I-75, there is a street marker that says "Flatwoods Park" on the northwest side of the road. This is the south entrance.

The north trailhead is east of I-75 on the south side of Bruce B. Downs. There is also ex-tensive bicycle path along Bruce B. Downs. *Managed by: Hillsborough County.*

Top: **cypress swamp at Flatwoods Park.**

Below: **skater at Flatwoods Park.**

71

PC

FORT COOPER STATE PARK
(Citrus County, 700 acres, hiking)

For a brief period during the Second Seminole War, US soldiers in dire straits took shelter on the banks of spring-fed Lake Holathlikaha. More than a century later, there are 3 miles of hiking trails through hardwood hammock, some near the lake, with more trails planned for the future. From I-75, take SR-44 west to Inverness, and turn south on US-41. Turn east on Eden Drive, just before passing the city limits. Then make a right after a short distance on Old Floral City Road. The entrance is one mile on the south side of the road.

FORT DESOTO PARK
(Pinellas County, 900 acres, bicycling and hiking)

This much-loved park receives tremendous recreational use. Located at the southern tip of a heavily populated county, the park and its beaches are almost always busy, particularly on weekends. The park has a beautiful view of the Sunshine Skyway Bridge which connects Pinellas to Manatee County. The paved paths are used by bicyclists, joggers, walkers, and roller bladers, while the beaches provide beach walks and swimming. It is possible to achieve 13 miles of paved distance, plus the 7-mile beach walk. Kayaks and canoes can be paddled through the inland mangroves and are available from a private outfitter. In St. Petersburg, from I-275, take the Bayway exit west and follow the signs. *Managed by: Pinellas County.*

Top, left: the Sunshine Skyway Bridge as seen from Fort Desoto Park.
Bottom, left: mangroves at Fort Desoto Park.
Bottom, right: steadying hands for a beginning roller blader.
Opposite page, top, left and right: a bicycle parking sign and the historic lighthouse, both in Boca Grande.
Opposite page, center: Boca Grande's rail-to-trail.

FLYING EAGLE
(Citrus County, 11,000 acres, multi-use)

Bordered by the Tsala Apopka Chain of Lakes and the Withlacoochee River, this land is in the midst of beautiful country. There are 15 miles of multi-use trails and overnight camping with permit.

While some land is former pasture or cleared, there are scenic sections, particularly at the bridge near the entrance. Alligators, turtles, and water moccasins can be seen in the picturesque creek, all cast in green by both growing algae and the reflection of some very tall cypress.

Outside of hunting season, the user may well enjoy this area in solitude, undisturbed by another human being.

From I-75, take SR-44 west to Inverness, and take US-41 south to Eden Drive which is located just before the city limits. Take Eden Drive east until it stops at Moccasin Slough Gate.

Managed by: Southwest Florida Water Management District.

JP

PC

FORT DRUM MARSH CONSERVATION AREA

(Indian River County, 20,862 acres, multi-use)

This is the southernmost headwaters of the St. Johns River and is located immediately south of Blue Cypress Marsh Conservation Area. Perhaps 10 miles of multi-use trail are in the capable hands of Florida Trail Association volunteers, including primitive camp sites. Stick Island, with no designated trails, is also open to hiking and equestrian use. In addition to the levee trails, there are wandering footpaths throughout the area. Habitats: flatwoods, floodplain, marsh, prairies, and swamp. From I-95 near Paradise Park, go west on SR-60 for 16 miles. Access is 10 miles east of Yeehaw Junction. Yeehaw Junction is also an exit of the Florida Turnpike. *Managed by: St. Johns River Water Management District.*

FORT PIERCE INLET STATE RECREATION AREA/ JACK ISLAND STATE PRESERVE

(St. Lucie County, 970 acres, bicycling and hiking)

The recreation area is on the beach, while the preserve is "across the street" on the Indian River. In addition to the beach and adjoining Pepper Beach, there is a nature trail, a coastal hammock, and mangroves. The Preserve is a mangrove island of 600 acres and has a 4.4-mile loop trail, popular with bicyclists and hikers. From US-1 in Ft. Pierce, take the North Beach Causeway to A1A, and go north 1.5 miles.

FRIENDSHIP TRAIL

(Hillsborough and Pinellas counties)

The older span of the Gandy Bridge, across almost 9 miles of Tampa Bay, was not torn down; rather it was turned into a bicycle and hiking trail. No shade, but plenty of bay, so take a hat, sunscreen, and water in all Florida seasons.

A tragic accident took the life of a rollerblader a few months after the trail opened. It emphasized the importance of wearing a helmet, and using caution coming down the hump. There have been a number of lesser injuries on this heavily-used recreational span.

In Tampa, from I-275, take Dale Mabry south to Gandy Boulevard, and proceed west. On the St. Petersburg side, from 4th Street turn east on Gandy Boulevard. Both trailheads are on the north side of the road by the old span. Plans are in the works to connect this trail, possibly through Weeden Island Preserve, to the Pinellas Trail, and to trails in Hillsborough County.

Managed by: Hillsborough and Pinellas counties.

GASPARILLA ISLAND STATE RECREATION AREA

(Lee County, 144 acres)

There is a very well-maintained trail approaching 7 miles for bicycling and foot traffic. It is built along the old railroad track that passes through Boca Grande, leading to the phosphate docks and the historical lighthouse at the south end of the island.

Jose Gaspar, for whom the island is named, is a mythical pirate. In less sophisticated times, locals had fun with Yankee tourists by selling treasure maps to Gaspar's alleged buried trunks of doubloons. In its Gasparilla Festival, Tampa annually celebrates a Gaspar invasion that never happened. Ye Mystic Krewe, a fraternal order made up mostly of the city's movers and shakers, invades the city. The locals surrender and the pirates are given the key to the city.

Don't miss the Boca Grande Lighthouse Museum. It is open Wednesday through Sunday from 10 am to 4 pm. There is much of interest here including a history of Boca Grande, information on the old railroad and fishing industries, and a self-guided lighthouse tour.

From I-75 near Venice, go south (the road appears to be going west) on River Road. After 4 miles, cross US-41 and continue on CR-777 to Englewood. Go south on CR-775A to CR-775 and continue south to Placida. Turn west and proceed over the toll causeway to Gasparilla Island and Boca Grande.

GREEN SWAMP
(Lake, Polk, and Sumter counties)

Historically, the Green Swamp was a very large area, perhaps 545,000 acres. It is the headwaters for the Hillsborough, Peace, and Withlacoochee rivers.

The habitats include flatwoods, floodplain, hardwood hammocks, lakes, marsh, ponds, prairie, river, scrub, and swamp.

The area is defined by the Brooksville, Lakeland, Lake Wales, and Winter Haven ridges, which were actually ancient islands during glacial periods of higher sea level. A portion of the Brooksville Ridge can be observed from I-75 north of Tampa. The Lake Wales Ridge is pronounced around the town of Clermont.

Florida Trail Association volunteers maintain two long Green Swamp trails, the east and west. The **Green Swamp East** Trail is 13 miles, with an 8-mile loop option, and the west is 21 miles. One trailhead of the East Trail is reached by traveling northeast of Lakeland 8 miles on US-98 to Rock Ridge Road, then going north for 10 miles.

Green Swamp West is perhaps best accessed at the Withlacoochee River Park (see separate account, this section, for directions).

There are over 40 miles of off-road bicycle trails through the Green Swamp, some on service roads. A map is a fine idea as these are lonely areas, with confusing loops and cross paths and roads. Maps can be obtained from the Southwest Florida Water Management District. Florida Trail maps can be obtained from the association.

Top: inside a cypress dome in the Green Swamp.

Bottom: a small portion of the Green Swamp during the rainy season.

GUM SLOUGH
(Sumter County, 4,000+ acres, multi-use)

This was formerly called the Carlton Tract and the old name might be restored in the future. It is located along the east bank of the Withlacoochee across from Potts Preserve. This is exceptionally beautiful land, particularly the hardwood areas, but there are also creeks, pine flatwoods, floodplain, marsh, and river.

On its southern border, Gum Slough abuts Half Moon Wildlife Management Area. A connecting trail is in progress and will result in 10 miles of hiking loop through both units. Shorter mileage options are also being planned. The two connected trails are intended for multi-use. However this is presently in the initial development stage, so it would be best to inquire.

From I-75, take SR-44 west toward Inverness. After 10 miles, turn north on CR-247 to Half Moon Wildlife Management Area. Park at the entrance gate and proceed. The Gum Slough property can also be reached by canoe or kayak from the Withlacoochee River.

Managed by: Southwest Florida Water Management District.

HALF MOON WILDLIFE MANAGEMENT AREA
(Sumter County, 9,300+ acres, multi-use)

There are over 9 miles of unimproved roads in excellent condition. For directions, ecosystems, and trails see the Gum Slough account above. *Managed by: Florida Fish and Wildlife Conservation Commission.*

HALPATA TASTANAKI PRESERVE
(Sumter County, 8,090 acres, multi-use)

This tract, named for a Seminole Chief, is adjacent to the Cross Florida Greenway and across SR-200 from Ross Prairie State Forest. These three areas form a recreational "hub."

Halpata Tastanaki has very good grass roads for bicycling and is multi-use. Be sure to follow the loop trail to the Withlacoochee River for a beautiful view. Slash pine on this property is being harvested, and it may be replaced with longleaf. Wiregrass restoration is in progress in places. This land is newly opened for public use, and recreational trails are being created. There is extensive road.

The preserve is not marked in any way from the highways. From I-75, go west on CR-484. Cross SR-200. The entrance is several miles farther west at 15410 SW Highway, an address found presently only on a mailbox. It is a 1-mile drive south to the trailhead.

Managed by: Southwest Florida Water Management District.

HAL SCOTT REGIONAL PRESERVE AND PARK
(Orange County, 8,427 acres, multi-use)

This is flatwoods and prairie along the Econlockhatchee River. There are 15 miles of multi-use trails, which can be done in 4.4, 10, and 11-mile loops, or the full 15. The 4.4-mile loop is maintained by Florida Trail volunteers. Primitive camping is available in designated areas.

During the week when recreational use is low, the visitor is likely to feel like lord and master of the entire preserve. This solitutde provides excellent opportunities for observing the natural behavior of wildlife, undisturbed by humans. Bald eagles, caracaras, deer, otters, pigs, sandhill cranes, turkeys, and wood storks can often be seen. A small colony of red-cockaded woodpeckers lives in the flatwoods.

From Orlando's Bee Line Expressway, exit at Meredith/Dallas. The entrance is on Dallas, 1.6 miles north of the intersection, on the west side of the road. The Meredith/Dallas exit is east of Orlando.

Managed by: St. Johns River Water Management District.

Top, left: treefrogs on a leaf in the Green Swamp.

Top, right: the intense red of the cardinal flower which can be found along river banks in Central, North, and Northwest Florida.

BLAZING

Many of Florida's trails are blazed, or marked, to keep hikers from getting lost. Many places follow the system of the Florida Trail which marks the main trail with orange paint. The markings are placed on trees, posts and poles. A double blaze means that the direction of the trail has changed. The Florida Trails Association recommends spotting the next blaze before making the turn. Blue blazes in the Florida Trail system are used to indicate side trails to campsites or when there are two trails. Some places with more than two trails blaze the third trail with white or yellow. On very long hikes thorugh dense habitats, blazing can make the difference between an enjoyable trek and becoming lost.

THE TROUBLE WITH PIGS

Florida's feral pigs add excitement and headaches along the trails. They are "cute" as piglets, appearing in amazing color variations, even orange. Sometimes the young look like someone has taken a paint brush to them. Adult pigs, however, are probably only cute to another pig.

For such a large mammal, normally 100 to 200 pounds (sometimes more) pigs reproduce very rapidly, with two litters per year and four to six piglets each litter.

Florida's pig population probably first began when the animals were taken along as dinner on the hoof by conquistadors and explorers, like DeSoto. Their numbers have been supplemented over the centuries by farm escapees, and the wild pig presence is now felt in over 20 states.

Pigs root up the earth in search of tasty plants and tubers, and generally annihilate what they eat, root and all. Many species of plants have been severely reduced by the activity of wild pigs. They also reduce available food for native animals.

Trappers are called-in at times at parks, recreation areas, and other public lands. The pigs may be taken to wildlife management areas, where they can be hunted. At times, farmers and frustrated wildlife officials have embarked on nightmarish campaigns to purge pigs from the wilderness.

The idea of putting contraceptives in feed for wild pigs has been suggested. It would seem fast, efficient, and less labor intensive. Some people have expressed concerns the contraceptives could have unexpected results (perhaps on bear), but in a time when even the food we eat is genetically altered, it would seem that a swine-specific contraceptive could be developed. Similar contraceptives have been used with some success to thin deer populations in the Northeast.

But perhaps there is another reason contraceptives are not considered. Feral pigs are good business for some. Trappers get paid, and some frustrated officials say off the record that perhaps some trappers take as few females as possible. Sold to farms, feral pigs bring a fair price. Wild pigs are even in demand for export to Europe, where they are considered something of a delicacy.

HICKORY HAMMOCK
(Highlands County, 9,487 acres, multi-use)

Hickory Hammock has a hiking trail of 7.9 miles, including 2.7 in open pasture. The area permits equestrian use. Habitats: floodplain, hardwood hammock, the Kissimmee River, and scrub. The trailhead is a parking lot on the north side of US-98 to the west of Okeechobee. The trailhead is on US-98 at the Istokpoga Canal. This is to the east of Lake Istokpoga, and to the east of CR-621.

Three miles further down Bluff Hammock is access to 40.8 miles of the Florida Trail. This segment stretches from Hickory Hammock Road to the Okeetantee State Recreation Area, and includes portions on levees along the Kissimmee River leading to the Okeechobee segments. At the present time, a section of private property has been closed on the Florida Trail section described above. There are plans to re-route the trail directly north and eliminate the Bluff Hammock Road walk. Until that occurs, the only real trailhead is on US-98.

Managed by: South Florida Water Management District.

Top, left: the Hillsborough Rapids, Hillsborough River State Park.
Top, right: a roadway in Highlands Hammock.
Above, left: suspension bridge across the river at Hillsborough River State Park.
Opposite page: gorgeous Flint Creek, a tributary of the Hillsborough River.

HIGHLANDS HAMMOCK STATE PARK
(Highlands County, 5,440 acres, multi-use)

The main attraction of Highlands Hammock is the hardwood forest where some huge oaks approach ages of 1,000 years. It is a joy to wander the shady trails, with thick palms, palmettos, and hardwoods.

Trails for walking/hiking total 10 miles, and many are a relaxing half-mile journey. There is a popular bicycling loop of 8 miles, and 11 miles for horseback riding. The park has a large campground with hookups as well as primitive camping.

In addition to the hardwood hammock, there are pine flatwoods, marsh, scrub, and swamp. There is a wonderful, long boardwalk over a section of cypress swamp, where a Florida cottonmouth might be seen swimming. There are plentiful alligators, and there have been Florida panther sightings. A herd of deer is usually seen easily in early morning or evening. Fox squirrels live in the trees.

Highlands Hammock is the administrative unit in charge of Lake June in Winter Scrub State Park, located in Lake Placid, on US-27 about 20 minutes south of Sebring. At present, there is only a short nature trail of less than a mile near Lake June in Winter.

Highlands Hammock is west of Sebring. From US-27 in Sebring, take CR-634 west, following the well-placed signs.

HILLSBOROUGH RIVER STATE PARK
(Hillsborough County, 2,900 acres, bicycling and hiking)

The trail along the Hillsborough River, including a suspension bridge, is approximately 3 miles, but can be made much longer by taking less obviously marked footpaths. It includes a view of the Hillsborough rapids, often photographed because of their obvious beauty.

A longer trail of 5 miles is being connected by a 6.5-mile trail to Sergeant Park, a Hillsborough County park (see separate account, this section). This is part of the Old Fort King Trail leading to Fort Dade, a military outpost during settler times. Upon completion, this will make a one way trip of 11.5 miles, or more if the state park is explored.

Bicycles can be ridden on the paved roads. Canoes can be rented within the park for a 3.5-hour journey on the river. This is a popular park for camping. It is also a place where residents from as far away as Tampa come to walk their dogs in the woods. Equestrian facilities are planned in conjunction with the Fort King Trail, but at present there are no equestrian activities.

Habitats: pine flatwoods, floodplain, hardwood hammock, marsh, prairie, river, and swamp.

On US-301, north of Tampa, and prominently announced by signs.

JACK CREEK
(Highlands County, 1,259 acres, hiking)

This area is mostly scrub on the Lake Wales Ridge. The only recreational activity allowed is hiking, and this is a little tough because the only roads are sugar sand. There are rare cutthroat grass seeps and scrub-jays. Josephine Creek runs into the area from Lake Josephine to the north, and feeds Jack Creek and a small lake. Jack Creek flows south into Lake Francis. From US-27, 5 miles north of Lake Placid, take Sebring Lakes Boulevard west through a series of bends and road name changes until reaching Jack Creek. *Managed by: Southwest Florida Water Management District.*

Left: **royal terns along the beach at Hobe Sound National Wildlife Refuge.**

HOBE SOUND NATIONAL WILDLIFE REFUGE
(Martin County, 967 acres, hiking)

The 3 miles of pristine beach adjoin another 3 miles to the north at St. Lucie State Park, combining for a grand 6-mile beach walk in sea turtle nesting country. Behind the beach is a twisting trail through the back dunes. In the winter months, a variety of gulls, sandpipers, and terns congregate and skitter along the shore.

The refuge office is on US-1 across from the entrance to Jonathan Dickinson State Park in Hobe Sound. There is a short 0.5-mile nature trail at the headquarters.

For the beach: from I-95, take SR-708 east through Hobe Sound, and go east 1.5 miles on North Beach Road until it dead-ends. Going south for 7 miles on SR-707 will lead to the Nature Conservancy's Blowing Rocks Preserve. Take the short nature walk to view the famous limestone outcrops, which are named for the way the sea rushes through "blow holes" in the rock, soaring high into the air when the surf is up.

HONEYMOON ISLAND STATE RECREATION AREA
(Pinellas County, 400 acres, bicycling and hiking)

Before Honeymoon Island was connected to the mainland by a causeway, about the only use this barrier island west of Dunedin had was by high school students with romance in mind. Actually, Honeymoon Island first received its name when a developer ran an ad in Life Magazine in the early 1940's promoting the island as a honeymoon spot.

Unfortunately, opening the island by bridge brought on a period of dredging and development, that (when thankfully stopped) left a partially denuded island with concrete chunks strewn up and down what had been a first class beach. Since 1982, the damage has been slowly reversed, and the concrete remnants removed.

A hike along the entire Honeymoon beach is easily a 3-mile trip one way. Osprey and Pelican Cove trails can be combined for a trip of 3-4 miles. Along the way, osprey might be seen nesting in the trees. Ospreys migrate to South America but always return to the same nest. If the nest is destroyed, they will build a new nest nearby. Great horned owls are also seen nesting here. A sign before the trail warns that rattlesnakes are present on the island.

South of Tarpon Springs, north of Dunedin, accessed from Alternate US-19, by going west on SR-586, prominently announced by signs. (There is an approximate 2.5-mile, paved path from the recreation area that adjoins the Pinellas Trail. Bicycles can be ridden on the island's sandy nature trails and on the paved roads.)

HONTOON ISLAND STATE PARK
(in the St. Johns River, on the border of Lake and Volusia counties, 1,650 acres, bicycling and hiking)

It is a stone throw from the mainland to this island in the St. Johns and Huntoon Dead rivers. Five miles of old roads, perfect for bicycling, pass through flatwoods and hammock, to end at picturesque river overlooks. Hiking is allowed there and on a 3-mile hiking-only trail. All trails depart from the campground and picnic area. There are six cabins available by reservation, and camping is allowed on the island. Many go over to picnic, bike, hike, or merely idle the day away.

Take SR-44 for 6 miles west from Deland, then CR-4410 south to the parking lot. During operating hours, boat transportation is usually standing by at the marina.

SNAKE BOOTS

Many beginning Florida hikers ask if they will need snake boots. This involves two important questions for those who hike along Florida trails. The first question is snakes, and the second is what to wear on your feet.

Although the chance of being bitten by a venomous snake is very unlikely, it is certainly wise to be able to identify Florida's venomous snakes, because snake bite does happen once in a blue moon. When it does, it is often unfortunately young children who stumble onto the snake unaware, or pick it up, not knowing the danger.

On rare occasions, snake bites have happened around homes. The eastern coral snake burrows beneath many Florida yards, and eastern diamondbacks have surprised homeowners outside or in a garage. Pygmy rattlesnakes have bitten shoppers in garden supply areas, and Florida cottonmouths (water moccasins) have struck children who stepped on them in picnic areas.

In the event of any snake bite, seek medical care immediately. In these days of antivenin and antibiotics, few need to worry if medical treatment is prompt.

Snake boots are not necessary to go hiking in Florida except for people who are unduly afraid of snakes. Certain workers walking through overgrown or flooded areas might need snake boots, but for hiking Florida's trails, wear what is most comfortable on the feet. Hiking long distances will cause great discomfort if the shoes are not good quality.

What is the best footwear for hiking? Some prefer special hiking shoes, others various athletic shoes, such as gym or jogging shoes. What is important on long walks is comfort and avoidance of injury.

Many scientists seek venomous snakes in Florida to observe their behavior, and it is usually difficult to find them. Herpetologists coming to Florida to find diamondbacks sometimes return home disappointed.

PC

JAY BLANCHARD PARK/LITTLE ECON GREENWAY
(Orange County, 412 acres, multi-use)

Jay Blanchard is a linear park along the Little Econ River. There is a paved path 4 miles one way, popular for bicycling and walking. The bike trail is on the south bank, and the equestrian trail on the north bank of the river. To the east of Orlando, from SR-50, go 1 mile north on Dean Road. The East-West Expressway crosses SR-50 in the middle of the trail. The trailhead is a short distance west of the expressway. *Managed by: Orange County.*

JONATHAN DICKINSON STATE PARK
(Martin County, 11,500 acres, bicycling and hiking)

This park is named for a shipwrecked Quaker who was stranded with his family among hostile Native Americans more than three centuries ago.

Just off busy US-1 are ancient sand dunes in a scrub habitat dotted with sand pine and rosemary. The dunes are most scenic near the entrance and around the observation tower on Hobe Mountain. Scrub-jays can be seen. There are also pine flatwoods, marsh, swamp, and a portion of one of the most attractive rivers in Florida, the Loxahatchee. The river is a wonderful canoe or kayak journey.

The paved bicycle trail is 3 miles. The hiking trails are: East Loop, 9.4 miles; Kitching Creek, 3.9 miles; and the Kitching Creek return, 1.2 miles. Directions to trailheads can be obtained at the gate or in the park brochure. The park has two campgrounds.

From the concession, a boat tour takes visitors up river to the former home of Trapper Nelson. On the river, there is usually an abundance of turtles, alligators, birds, and sometimes manatees. Trapper Nelson was a rugged individualist who lived and made his living out of the wilderness, and who died under mysterious circumstances.

From I-95, take the Hobe Sound Exit east to US-1, then go south for 6 miles.

KICCO WILDLIFE MANAGEMENT AREA
(Polk and Osceola counties, 7,500 acres, hiking)

The name is an abbreviation of the Kissimmee Island Cattle Company, in existence during World War I and into the Great Depression of the 1930s. It is not pronounced *key-co* as one would think, but instead is pronounced *kiss-oh*.

This area is mostly floodplain, marsh, and the river. It has a 9.5-mile hiking trail and access to 27 adjacent miles of the Florida Trail. Camping is allowed by permit.

Two areas with great names are along the trail: Ice Cream Slough and Rattlesnake Hammock Marsh. The marsh has been restored from cow pasture. There are many theories as to how Ice Cream Slough got its name. One guess: hiking past it in August creates a serious craving for something really cold and sweet.

Go west from the Florida Turnpike at Yeehaw Junction on SR-60, for the access road to River Ranch Resort. The access road to Kicco is off River Ranch Road.

Managed by: Florida Fish and Wildlife Conservation Commission.

Top: a jogger on the trail in Jonathan Dickinson State Park. This portion of the trail is a scrub area with sand pine.

Bottom: a scene along Kitching Creek Trail in Jonathan Dickinson State Park.

KISSIMMEE PRAIRIE STATE PRESERVE
(Okeechobee County, 46,000 acres, multi-use)

For those seeking wilderness, here is an amazing 75 square miles of it, including 70 miles of multi-use trails, and six primitive campsites. There are plenty of wild animal encounters here, whether it be a young alligator walking down the road near a marsh, a hawk swooping down on prey, or deer bolting off through the prairie.

Prairie is one of the vanishing Florida ecosystems. Once vast in this part of Florida, prairie is now reduced to a number of small pockets. In portions of the preserve, it is still possible to look out over miles of remaining prairie, a very unique view. Other habitats include floodplain, hammock, marsh, and the Kissimmee River.

A map is available from the preserve headquarters. Calling in advance, particularly for primitive camping, is a wise idea since this area is newly opened to recreation and much may still be in flux.

Traveling northwest on US-98/SR-700 from Okeechobee, the preserve is to the north of the small community of Basinger. Take SR-700A north, and follow the well-placed directional signs for 9 miles to the entrance.

LAKE APOPKA RESTORATION AREA
(Lake and Orange counties, 20,068 acres, bicycling and hiking)

It is amazing how differently two people can view the same land. One writer and photographer joked that because of Apopka's history of pollution, its rough condition, and closures for restoration work, this place should not be recommended. Yet one of the state's foremost scientists insisted that this area should be visited because it offers a good lesson that once nature is devastated, it is costly and difficult, sometimes impossible, to restore.

Lake Apopka, the 4th largest lake in Florida, is roughly 7% the size of Lake Okeechobee. Lake Apopka has long been known for its pollution, and more than once was described as the most polluted lake in Florida. Efforts to improve it have been underway since 1987. Its problems were caused by sewage, agricultural waste from the citrus industry, and muck farming. As a consequence, Apopka developed a severe weed problem, becoming clogged with eelgrass, pondweed, and water hyacinths. The lake became increasingly eutrophic, that is, rich in nutrients, but poor in oxygen.

Recreational trails for bicyclists and hikers are 6-7 miles long, complete with observation platforms, and are on the southwestern corner of the acquired lands. From the platforms, it is possible to overlook the lake and also see a substantial variety of birds.

Go north from Clermont on US-27, turn northeast onto CR-561, and then east on CR-48. Proceed south on Ranch Road for 2-3 miles. This is a paved road that quickly becomes dirt. The road makes a number of turns before the St. Johns River Water Management District signs begin to appear.

LAKE ARBUCKLE STATE FOREST
(see Lake Wales Ridge State Forest)

LAKE JESSUP WILDERNESS AREA
(Seminole County, 490 acres, multi-use)

There are 3 miles of trails located on the north shore of Lake Jessup which is south of Sanford. Habitats: floodplain, hammock, lake, marsh, and swamp. From I-4, take Lake Mary Boulevard east to Sanford Avenue, then go south to the entrance at Lake Jessup Park.

Managed by: Seminole County.

LAKE KISSIMMEE STATE PARK
(Polk County, with a sliver of Osceola County, 5,000 acres. bicycling and hiking)

The park is near the 35,000-acre lake that is its namesake. This is one of Florida's premier state parks because of the plentiful wildlife easily observed. Birds seen during a typical visit may include barred owls, bobwhite quail, bald eagles, sandhill cranes, scrub-jays, and turkeys. At times, whooping cranes from the Three Lakes Wildlife Management Area show up, particularly if there has been fire in the flatwoods. With hunting banned for more than two decades, white-tailed deer seem everywhere, and it is not unusual to see dozens in a day.

Hiking: two loop trails, Buster Island, 6.2 miles, and North Loop, 5.6. A third trail, 1.1 mile each way in and out, departs from the North Loop, and is named Gobbler Ridge Trail. Bicycling: on the 3 mile paved road from the gate. Primary habitats: flatwoods, prairie, lake, and scrub, with some marsh and swamp.

Go east from Lake Wales 6 miles on SR-60, then north on Boy Scout Road/Camp Mack Road, and follow the signs. When the road comes to a stop sign, turn east or right, and proceed 4 miles.

Top: autumn on Buster Island Tail, Lake Kissimmee State Park.
Above: couple examining a large oak on the Buster Island Trail.

LAKE LOUISA STATE PARK
(Lake County, 4,372 acres, equestrian and hiking)

From CR-561 south of Clermont, there are two entrances; one leads to Lake Louisa, while the other leads to 19 miles of trails in four loops on the Central Ridge.

The lake has gnarled cypress along the shore. In the drought of 2000, the shore increased perhaps the length of a football field as the water level dropped.

Starting from Clermont on SR-50, go south on CR-561 for 7 miles, then east on Lake Nellie Road to the entrance. An alternative entrance is on US-27, 12 miles south of Clermont.

LAKE MARION CREEK MANAGEMENT AREA
(Polk County, 4,000 acres, bicycling and hiking)

To the north of Lake Marion, this area has two trails. The Snell Creek Trail is approximately one mile in and one mile out, and is far too sandy for even a 21-gear mountain bike. The Huckleberry Island Trail is 2.5 miles in and 2.5 miles out, and firmer for bicycling. The trails pass through mixed habitats: pine woods, creek, seasonal lakes, and marsh, but do not reach 2,990-acre Lake Marion, located to the south. There are some unannounced forks, and no blazes, but with a little trial-and-error, the trail will not be lost. There is a primitive camping site on the Huckleberry Island Trail which requires a permit. From US-17/92 in Haines City, go east on CR-580 for 4 miles. There are prominent signs on the road. *Managed by: South Florida Water Management District.*

LAKE MINNEOLA SCENIC TRAIL
(Lake County, bicycling and hiking)

This rail-to-trail is hard to miss in downtown Clermont, and is busy most days. It runs from the historic district to nearby Minneola, a bit to the north, where it is equally conspicuous. Along the west side of the 3.1-mile trail is pretty Lake Minneola, usually bathed in sunshine. From SR-50 in Clermont simply follow the signs. Minneola can be reached from US-27, 1.5 miles north of SR-50. *Managed by: Lake County.*

LAKE PANASOFFKEE PROJECT
(Sumter County, 9,550 acres, multi-use)

The floodplain here which still remains in a natural state is a glorious sight–a dark tangle of trees and vegetation with fleeting glimpses of wildlife.

Lake Panasoffkee is a popular fishing lake and campground area, but often it is hard to get a good look without putting in a boat. In many places, Panasoffkee's floodplain has been reduced or even cleared. For Florida, it is a large lake at 4,460 acres.

Heavily vegetated floodplains are valuable in many ways, not just for their beauty. In addition to providing homes for wildlife, they slow storm water runoff, giving the water time to percolate–a natural retention system.

Before the water management district acquired this land, it was used for wintering racehorses. There are 18 miles of equestrian trails (also open for hiking), as well as eight horse stalls available on a first-come basis. Bicycling, though arduous, is allowed on the North Loop Trail, and south to Little Jones Creek. In addition to primitive camping, it is also possible to camp with your horse with permit. With limited present use, this is like having your own personal kingdom. As an example, on tax day (April 15, 2000), there were a total of three individual sign-ins for that entire month to date.

The floodplain can also be viewed from the comfort of a car near the south gate at the end of Warm Springs Road, about 2 miles west from US-301 in Coleman. The main entrance is marked by large arches on the south side of SR-44, 2 to 3 miles west of I-75 from Wildwood. *Managed by: Southwest Florida Water Management District.*

LAKE PROCTOR WILDERNESS AREA
(Seminole County, 475 acres, multi-use)

There are 6 miles of trails, some in loops, in the flatwoods, hammocks, and sandhill around scenic Lake Proctor. Take SR-46 east from Sanford, and follow it to the entrance on the north side, 1 mile east of CR-426, near Geneva. *Managed by: Seminole County.*

Top: **Lake Louisa near Clermont.**

PC

LAKE WALES RIDGE STATE FOREST
(Polk County, 20,242 acres, multi-use)

Formerly Lake Arbuckle State Forest, this large forest is divided into two tracts: Lake Arbuckle (13,531 acres) and Walk-in-the-Water (6,711 acres).

LAKE ARBUCKLE TRACT

No nature enthusiast should miss the Lake Arbuckle Tract since it offers arguably the best example of scrub habitat on the Lake Wales Ridge. In the last period of global warming, this land served as a life-sheltering island standing above sea level.

This is one of Florida's treasures, although little visited, and perhaps unappreciated. Most of the typical plants (and many of the rare ones) found in Central Ridge scrub grow here. Scrub is often indicated by sand pine and Florida rosemary; both are here, including very tall sand pines near Reedy Creek. Black racers, indigo snakes, and scrub-jays are often seen, along with pigs, deer, and an occasional bear.

Below the pines in some of the flatwoods, rare cutthroat grass has choked out palmettos. Cutthroat is found only on the ridge seepage areas, and one other small area in South Florida. It is very sharp on the edges, and can inflict a cut like paper.

This is challenging hiking, both because of the 20.2-mile length and the amount of deep white sand and pig-rutted earth; the walk can be shortened to 11 miles by cutting across the loop on Godwin Trail. The section along Reedy Creek overlooks this small stream from a height of perhaps 30 feet, fairly high for Central Florida. This high spot is astride the Lake Wales Ridge. There is primitive overnight camping by permit for those who wish to break the trip into two days.

School Bus Road is a north-south graded limerock road through the tract. It is the only possibility for bicycling. It is 5 miles long, so a round trip yields 10 miles. While there is an old railroad bed that would be passable by bike, most of the loop is very sandy, and portions of it would not allow a tractor, much less a bike.

Equestrian opportunities are permitted on all roads and fire breaks, but not on the hiking trails.

From US-27/98 in Avon Park, go 6 miles east on CR-64. The marked entrance to School Bus Road is on the north side.

WALK-IN-THE-WATER TRACT

This tract is between Tiger Creek Preserve to the north and the Lake Arbuckle Tract to the south. Both tracts have substantial flatwoods and scrub, but this tract is more hilly, with some interesting views.

Florida Trail volunteers have built a 2.8-mile loop trail with a trailhead along CR-630. Two more trails (5 and 9 miles) are planned. Perhaps 20-25 miles of equestrian roads are in the tract, and the equestrian trailhead is on Walk-in-the-Water Road.

Walk-in-the-Water Road goes south from SR-60, east of Lake Wales about 8 miles. The tract is to the west along Walk-in-the-Water Road (at times, road signs have shortened the name to Walk-in-Water, but it is the same road). It meets CR-630 to the south.

Managed by: Division of Forestry.

Above: rare cutthroat grass has choked-out palmettos to dominate the flatwoods.

Below: a sandy trail in Lake Wales Ridge State Forest.

PC

LITTLE-BIG ECON STATE FOREST
(Seminole County, 5,045 acres, multi-use)

The purchase of this forest land was begun in 1994, and a total of over 15,500 acres are slated for acquisition. The forest takes its name from the Econlockhatchee and Little Econlockhatchee rivers.

The unit presently exists in two separate tracts: the Demetree and Kilbee. Kilbee is on the banks of the St. Johns, with a trail that is approximately 1.5 miles each way. The Kilbee Trailhead is on the south side of SR-46, east from Geneva 4 miles. It is open only for hiking.

The Kolokee Loop is located in Demetree and has straight portions and loops approaching 6.2 miles. It is part of the Trailwalker Program. The loop is maintained by Florida Trail volunteers and has a trailhead with parking on the south side of CR-426 southwest of SR-46 and Geneva by 4 miles. This should not be confused with a nearby portion of the Florida Trail along CR-419 to the south.

The forest is multi-use, and primitive camping is allowed by permit. Separate bicycle and equestrian trailheads are off Snowhill Road (listed as SR-13 on some maps). They are on the west side of Snowhill Road, 3 and 4 miles south from the junction of CR-426 and SR-46 in Geneva. The forest office is also on Snowhill Road.

Managed by: Division of Forestry, St. Johns River Water Management District.

LITTLE MANATEE RIVER STATE RECREATION AREA
(Hillsborough County, 1,600 acres, multi-use)

To hike the 6.2-mile Florida Trail Loop, obtain a map and the key to the gate from the entrance kiosk. The key is necessary to open the gate to the parking area. Proceed north from the recreation area on US-301 to the trailhead on the west side of the road. This is an exceptionally scenic trail, especially along the Little Manatee River. Some local naturalists use the trail almost daily. An equestrian trail inside the recreation area is highly recommended by equestrian users and bicycling is allowed on the paved road.

Outside the recreation area, the Little Manatee River Canoe Outpost provides canoe and kayak rentals for those wishing to explore one of Florida's designated canoe trails. In times of high water, the river should only be attempted by experienced paddlers, as the river is not wide, the extra water makes it dangerouly high and fast, and there are overhanging obstacles. Otherwise, the river is scenic and pleasant with few hindrances.

Primary habitats: flatwoods, floodplain, river, and scrub dominated by sand pine.

From I-75, exit east on CR-674 to Sun City, then go south 4 miles on US-301, and west on Lightfoot Road a few hundred yards.

Top, left: Cypress Creek along the Loop Trail at Little Manatee River State Recreation Area.

Top, right: a duckweed-covered pond at Little Manatee River State Recreation Area.

Right, bottom: scrub, one of the main habitats at Little Manatee River State Recreation Area.

LOWER HILLSBOROUGH DETENTION AREA
(Hillsborough County, 17,000 acres, equestrian and hiking)

Many of the parks within this area are discussed separately, e.g. Dead River and Wilderness Park. Two equestrian gates into this area afford tremendous riding opportunities. The Oak Ridge Trail is near the northernmost end of Morris Bridge Road on the east side, with spacious accommodation for horse trailers. Morris Bridge becomes the extension of Fletcher Avenue going east from I-75 near Temple Terrace. Cow Horse Slough has another trail leading from Jefferson Road on the north side of Fowler Avenue east of I-75. Bicycling is not allowed in district areas with equestrian trails, but hiking is, and this area has many gorgeous places. *Southwest Water Management District.*

LOWER WEKIVA RIVER STATE PRESERVE
(Lake and Seminole counties, 17,000 acres, equestrian and hiking)

Fantastic trails within the preserve pass through sandhill and hammock. Along the way, the visitor is likely to see box turtles, deer, fox squirrels, and gopher tortoises. Longleaf pine, turkey oak, and wiregrass dominate the sandhill, with live oaks and palms in the hammocks.

The river is a spring-fed tributary of the St. Johns. A portion of the preserve touches on the St. Johns River, and the Wekiva River runs along the western edge of the preserve. Along its banks is a splendid land of floodplain, dark hammock, river, and swamp, where bears are occasionally seen.

The Wekiva River offers excellent canoe adventure. This area can be combined with Rock Springs Run State Reserve, Seminole State Forest, and Wekiwa Springs State Park to fill up a weekend or a month, depending on the amount of exploration and effort.

There are over 20 miles of trail, including four loops. It is thus wise to obtain a map before proceeding from Wekiwa Springs State Park.

The preserve is west of Sanford. From I-4, go west on SR-46 for 4 miles. The entrance is just east of the Wekiva River on the north side of the road.

MEDARD PARK
(Hillsborough County, 1,200 acres, equestrian)

This is a busy county park with popular campgrounds, picnic tables, and heavy use even during the week in summer. Medard would not be included in this book except for its equestrian use, as it has no discernible hiking trail, and only difficult bicycling on the busy road. There is a 3.25-mile bridle path described as taking three to four hours of riding time (presumably on a very slow horse). This path mostly follows the fence line. Two-thirds of the park is a reservoir in a former phosphate mine pit, with an island and observation tower at the end of a boardwalk. East of Brandon on SR-60, go south on Turkey Creek Road for 2 miles. SR-60 is an exit of I-75. *Managed by: Hillsborough County.*

Above: bicyclists on the Morris Bridge Trail.

Opposite page: St. Lucie Rocks Beach, Hutchinson Island, Port St. Lucie.

MERRITT ISLAND NATIONAL WILDLIFE REFUGE
(Brevard and Volusia counties, 140,000 acres, hiking)

This National Wildlife Refuge and Canaveral National Seashore are safety buffer zones for the space program, frequently closed during launches. Merritt is a barrier island, with coastal mangrove estuary along the Indian River, and beach on the Atlantic Ocean.

The 7-mile Black Point Wildlife Drive can be driven or hiked; the Cruickshank Trail 5-mile loop is located at Stop 8. Bird congregations are huge here during the winter migratory season. It is located 2 miles northeast of Titusville on CR-406.

Bicycling is not officially encouraged and is an issue under study. It might be forbidden if it is felt to conflict with the mission of the refuge. At present, bicyclists can ride not only the Black Point Wildlife Drive, but also both the Palm and Oak Hammock trails.

The headquarters is on CR-402, a road that splits from CR-406. At the headquarters, there is a short nature trail around a swamp, and on CR-402 there are two trails: Palm Hammock, 2 miles, and Oak Hammock, a half-mile. The Sandy Ridge Trail is also a half-mile, and is located off SR-3, 2 miles south of Haulover Canal. A map with all trail locations is available at the visitor's center.

Merritt Island, Canaveral National Seashore, and the Cape Kennedy Space Center can be combined for an interesting weekend.

From I-95, exit on Garden Street (SR-406) east. Cross the Indian River Lagoon, and follow the signs to the visitors center, four miles northeast of the bridge.

MORRIS BRIDGE BICYCLE AREA
(Hillsborough County, 112 acres, bicycling)

Although joggers and hikers use it, this section of the Wilderness Park Off-Road Trails has been created by bicyclists with other bicyclists in mind. It has some interesting segments with names like "Washboard," "Hog Wild," and "Gator Bait." It contains a number of intersecting and crossing trails on an approximate 5-mile track. It connects to Flatwoods Park through a series of trails exceeding 18 miles, but with off-shoots can become more than that. This area is one of Florida's premier bicycle rides, and draws bicyclists from afar. This area is used and maintained by the Southwest Association of Mountain Bike Pedallers (the SWAMP Club). From I-75 in Tampa, exit east on Fletcher Avenue, which becomes Morris Bridge Road. The entrance is less than a quarter mile east on the south side of the road. *Managed by: Hillsborough County.*

Top: a bicyclist admiring the resurrection fern on the canopy at Myakka River State Park.

Left: butterfly orchids growing on an oak tree.

Below: a trail through the treetops at Myakka River State Park.

MYAKKA RIVER STATE PARK
(Sarasota County, 28,750 acres, multi-use)

Myakka is Florida's largest state park, and combined with Myakka Prairie, covers more than 37,000 acres. It is also one of the most "complete" parks in Florida in terms of activities. It has recently added a short canopy boardwalk and a tower in the treetops.

The park is a favorite for all trail users, although some bicyclists feel the off-road trails are too sandy to enjoy. Equestrian users travel considerable distances to ride through its natural splendor. The park receives high numbers of all types of recreational visitors, and is an important link in educating the public concerning nature and the environment. It is one of those places worth a thousand mile drive. Both the river and the lake are popular for canoe and kayak outings, and 12 miles of the river are within the park. Primitive camping, campsites, and cabins are available, and there is a concession boat ride on the lake.

There are many habitats within Myakka. In addition to lake and river, there are pine flatwoods, floodplain, hardwood hammocks, marsh, prairie, and scrub.

Deer and raccoons are almost certain to be seen, and Myakka is well known for sandhill cranes. Large alligators are usually seen below the bridge that crosses the river in the park.

Bicycling: 7 miles paved, 50 unpaved miles. Equestrian: 12 miles. Hiking: 38 miles, including a Florida Trail portion.

Myakka is on the north side of SR-72, 9 miles east of I-75 from Sarasota.

Top, left: small, grassy airplants on trees at Myakka River State Park.

Above: yellow coreopsis blooming at Myakka River State Park.

Bottom: horse riders on the popular equestrian trails in Myakka River State Park.

MYAKKA PRAIRIE
(Sarasota County, 8,248 acres, bicycling and hiking)

These water management district lands are directly south of Myakka River State Park on SR-72 and open for hiking and bicycling only. As the name implies, this is a substantial prairie area, with pine flatwoods and marsh. Visitors must first check in at Myakka River State Park, on SR-72, 9 miles east of I-75 and Sarasota.

MYAKKA STATE FOREST
(Sarasota County, 8,000 acres, multi-use)

The forest includes North and South Loop trails of 5.4 and 7.4 miles, both included in the Trailwalker Program. Both loops are multi-use on old construction roads, and cars are not allowed. The entry roads present a challenge in both wet and dry seasons, and care is needed to avoid becoming stuck. From I-75 near North-port, take the River Road exit west and cross US-41. The forest entrance is on the south side of River Road perhaps 1 mile from US-41.

Managed by: Division of Forestry.

ORLANDO WETLANDS PARK/ ORLANDO WILDERNESS PRESERVE
(Seminole County, 1,650 acres, multi-use)

The older, superseded name is the Orlando Wilderness Park, and it has also been known s the Orlando Wilderness Preserve. Its primary mission is removing excess nutrients, particularly nitrogen and phosphorus, from reclaimed waste water before it passes into the St. Johns River. It is apparently successful in this mission since the waters it releases are lower in nutrient levels than the St. Johns itself.

There are over 18 miles of dike roads traversing the park. There are two other trails: a central birding trail 3.5 miles long and a meandering trail through hammock of 5 miles. Portions of the Florida Trail are located on the park property. Equestrian use is permitted throughout the park.

The park is closed from October 1 through January 20th of every year, but the Florida Trail segment remains open all year.

Travel east on SR-50 from Orlando. This state road can be accessed from the Bee Line Expressway, or from I-4. In the town of Christmas, turn north on Ft. Christmas Road and go 2.5 miles. Turn east on Wheeler Road and go 1.5 miles to the trailhead. There are commendably clear signs announcing the park.

Managed by: City of Orlando.

OSCAR SCHERER STATE PARK
(Sarasota County, 1,400 acres, bicycling and hiking)

In addition to a short trail along South Creek, there is substantial property east of the recreational area (across the railroad tracks), sufficient for even experienced hikers to get lost on occasion in the 15 miles of trails. This is a popular, full-facility campground, crowded and difficult to get into during the winter months. Primary habitats: flatwoods, marsh, river, and scrub with friendly scrub-jays. From I-75, take the Laurel/Nokomis exit west to US-41, and then go north 2.5 miles to the park entrance, prominently announced by a sign.

(FRED MARQUIS) PINELLAS TRAIL
(Pinellas County, bicycling and hiking)

This 50 mile rail-to-trail stretches south from Tarpon Springs to St. Petersburg. Ambitious plans were announced at the end of 1999 to add another 50 miles of trail by connecting it to power line rights-of way. Then it would also join the newly opened Friendship Trail over the old span of the Gandy Bridge, and the entire Pinellas Peninsula might be encircled by trail and joined to trails in neighboring Hillsborough.

This is a busy, urban rail-to-trail. It receives heavy use from bicyclists, hikers, joggers, and roller-bladers. Some interesting portions of it cross busy highways like Alternate US-19 via overpasses. As a place for recreation, like all rail-to-trails, it is blessing for the community.

It is best to access the northern portion of the trail in downtown Tarpon Springs near Alternate US-19. The trail in the south ends presently in St. Petersburg at Gibbs High School, also on Alternate US-19. There are many potential entry points, and a guide is available from Pinellas County (see Appendix for address).

Top: bicyclists traveling a portion of the Pinellas Trail near Tarpon Springs.

Above: this bridge on the Pinellas Trail crosses Alternate 19. The surface is a bit wavy, not flat, making for an exciting ride.

Left: a friendly scrub-jay about to open an acorn.

THE FIGHT OVER THE STATE BIRD

Attempts to replace the mockingbird with the scrub-jay as Florida's state bird have been turned back by the state legislature. Many strange reasons were given. Opponents called the scrub-jay a "welfare bird," because it is willing to take handouts of peanuts. These legislators seem much more comfortable with a bird that attacks cats, dogs, humans, and is found in many states of the eastern US instead of just in Florida.

POTTS PRESERVE
(Citrus County, 8,100+ acres, multi-use)

Florida Trail Association volunteers have created and maintained a terrific 17-mile loop. Twelve miles are open for equestrian use. The bicycling is on "roads" in the western section, but they are quite sandy in places, and not very enjoyable. No biking is allowed in the eastern section along the Withlacoochee River where the paths might support it better.

Overnight primitive camping is available by permit. There are several primitive camping areas, including one near the eastern trailhead on the banks of the Withlacoochee. It is perhaps one of the most heavily used primitive camping areas in the water management district simply because of the appealing location.

Probably half the trail is along the river, where there are towering, old oak trees. Among them are cypress, magnolia, and longleaf, pond, and slash pine. In spring and summer, the trees along the banks look like living walls, and it is difficult to pick out individual trees in the solid, radiant green.

Equestrian entrance: from Inverness, take CR-581, 6 miles northeast from US-41 to Dee River Ranch Road. The entrance is on the north side. Hiking entrance: located on the north side near the end of CR-581 just before the public boat ramp. CR-581 is a little tricky to follow at first. *Managed by: Southwest Florida Water Management District.*

Top: cypress knees along the Withlacoochee River (South) bordering Potts Preserve.

Above: canna lilies along the Florida Trail in Potts Preserve.

Middle, right: freshly mowed trail through the primitive campgrounds by the Withlacoochee River (South) in Potts Preserve.

Bottom, right: a volunteer from the Florida Trail Association blazing a trail through Potts Preserve.

PC

RIVER LAKES CONSERVATION AREA
(Brevard County, 14,000 acres, multi-use)

River Lakes Conservation Area is north of Three Forks Marsh Conservation Area and east of Viera, near Rockledge. The Moccasin Island Restoration Project was added to the conservation area in 1999. It has 4-6 miles of unimproved roadways through pasture and hammocks. The roads are drivable, however, visitors must park about one-third of the way in and access is by hiking, biking or horseback riding after that point. Access is still under construction, but the area is already informally open to the public. From I-95 south of Cocoa, go west on SR-520 (Fisk Boulevard) to Duda Ranch property signs, and continue beyond about 300 yards to the entrance. The Duda Ranch office is on the left.

ROCK SPRINGS RUN STATE RESERVE
(Orange and Seminole counties, 13,000 acres, multi-use)

There are parallel trails of 15 miles, one each for bicycling, hiking, and horse riding.

Rock Springs Run is named for a beautiful spring pouring forth out of a limestone wall. It makes a 7-mile run to the Wekiva River.

Habitats: flatwoods, ponds, river, scrub, and swamp. Deer and gopher tortoise are plentiful, and an occasional bear can be seen in the reserve.

The run is an excellent canoe/kayak journey. Primitive camping is available with permit. The Reserve can be combined with Wekiwa Springs State Park, Seminole State Forest, and Lower Wekiva State Preserve.

Thirty miles north of Orlando, exit I-4 west at Woodruff Springs on SR-46, then proceed to the entrance which is located on the south side of the road.

ROSS PRAIRIE STATE FOREST
(Marion County, 5,082 acres, equestrian and hiking)

This attractive sandhill forest was recovering from fire in April, 2000. Forestry information states that the only recreation is on the firebreak around the fence line. However, there are some excellent limestone and sand roads within the forest, certainly exceeding 5 miles. This area is newly acquired, in transition, and future trails are planned. The Cross Florida Greenway section of the Florida Trail is on adjoining greenway lands. From I-75 south of Ocala, go west on SR-200, across SR-484. The forest is on the south side of the road within a few miles. *Managed by: Division of Forestry.*

ST. SEBASTIAN RIVER BUFFER PRESERVE
(Brevard and Indian River counties, 21,951 acres, multi-use)

This place is a delightful surprise for those who like flatwoods and scrub, and who feel they have been everywhere, seen everything, and done it all. A first class job has been done on creating long loop trails and providing adequate trailhead parking for cars and horse trailers.

At the north entrance are as many as 19 miles of hiking trails, and there are two equestrian trails, one in the northeast and one in the south, with a combined mileage approaching 26.5 miles. The preserve brochure describes the bicycling conditions as "rugged." Keep your bike wheels on the road that runs the length of the preserve and passes under I-95, or you might find yourself carrying your bike more than riding it. Primitive camping is available at designated campsites.

Habitats: flatwoods, marsh, scrub, and swamp. Among the wildlife: manatees, red-cockaded woodpeckers, scrub-jays, and bald eagles.

From I-95, go east on SR-514 toward Malabar. After 1 mile, go south on CR-507 (Babcock Road), to Buffer Preserve Drive.

Managed by: St. Johns River Water Management District

ST. LUCIE INLET STATE PRESERVE
(Martin County, 928 acres, hiking).

St. Lucie abuts Hobe Sound National Wildlife Refuge. Its 2.7 miles of beach combined with the more than 3 miles at Hobe Sound, make the total hike about 6 miles. St. Lucie is either accessed from Hobe Sound or by boat.

(JOHN B.) SARGEANT PARK
(Hillsborough County, 423 acres)

Previously known as a canoe landing with a delightful 0.25-mile boardwalk, Sargeant Park is located where the Hillsborough River meets Flint Creek. This park is being connected to Hillsborough River State Park by a 6.5-mile multi-use trail, the Old Fort King Trail. Stables are planned at the edge of the state park, but horses are not allowed in that park and will be confined to the new trail when complete. From I-4 east of Tampa, exit on US-301 and go north. Located on US-301, northeast of Temple Terrace, 2 miles south of Hillsborough River State Park, on the west side of the road. *Managed by: Hillsborough County.*

SAVANNAS STATE RESERVE
(Martin County, 5,000 acres, bicycling and hiking)

In addition to having perhaps 8 miles of trail, and 5.5 miles of paved road for bikes, this is a popular area to canoe or kayak. Habitats: lake, marsh, river, and scrub with sand pine. South of Ft. Pierce and to the west of the Indian River. From US-1, north of Stuart, take CR-707 (Indian River Drive) to Riverview Drive, turn right, then go left on Gumbo Limbo Lane.

Top: **Rock Springs Run in Wekiva Springs State Park.**

SEBASTIAN INLET STATE RECREATION AREA
(Brevard County, 740 acres, hiking)

In addition to 3 miles of beach to walk, this barrier island has mangroves and hammock. There is a 1.5-mile hiking trail, and there are camping options. This is one of Florida's busiest recreation areas. On A1A, 15 miles south of Melbourne Beach.

SEMINOLE RANCH CONSERVATION AREA
(Brevard, Orange, Seminole, and Volusia counties, 28,785 acres, multi-use)

These are the first lands acquired under the "Save Our Rivers" Program. They include 12 miles of St. Johns River shoreline which is more than 90% floodplain with palm dominated hammocks, and a lesser amount of oak hammock. On one recent day, the only users were two fishermen in a boat at the landing on Hatband Road.

There are multi-use trails of at least 10 miles as well as 4.4 miles of the Florida Trail. It is also a good place to canoe on the St. Johns, and there is overnight camping with permit (a good supply of bug repellent is important).

Along SR-46, east of Oviedo, there are several gates on the south side of the road, with very limited parking. Turning south onto Hatband Road, there are more gates, including an equestrian gate with room for trailers. The area stretches south to SR-50, where the access gates have no visible parking.

Managed by: St. Johns River Water Management District.

SEMINOLE STATE FOREST
(Lake County, 19,284 acres, multi-use)

This is a fine place with many miles of wandering roads, and a 24-mile section of the Florida Trail known as Cassia. Two loop trails connecting to the forest go into the Lower Wekiva Preserve. To the south and slightly west of the preserve on SR-46 are the loops of Rock Springs Run and Wekiwa Springs State Park. There are over 20 miles of very firm roads for bicycling. Horseback riding is allowed on three loops: Paola (4.2 miles), River Creek (6.9 miles), and Sulfur Island (7.4 miles). A brochure containing a map is usually available at the entrance, or can be obtained in advance from Division of Forestry.

On a recent day, within just a few feet of the entrance to the forest, nature extended a welcome. Immediately, there were gopher tortoises, colorful wildflowers, and a hawk carrying off a black racer. Deer are plentiful within the forest, and bears are seen from time to time.

There is an entrance on the north side of SR-46 just west of the Wekiva River. Another entrance is on SR-44 to the west of I-4. There are trailheads at both entrances. *Managed by: Division of Forestry.*

SEMINOLE-WEKIVA TRAIL
(Seminole County, multi-use)

This paved path had its grand opening on September 9, 2000 and is a 14-mile, multi-use trail. From I-4 near Longwood, take SR-434 west to Douglas Avenue, turn left on Douglas, continue to North Street, and turn right. *Managed by: Seminole County.*

SPLIT OAK FOREST MITIGATION PARK
(Orange and Osceola counties, 1,689 acres, hiking, and equestrian by permit)

Four trails are maintained by Florida Trail volunteers: the North and South Red loops total 4.4 miles, the Gray Connector 0.9 miles, and the Moss Park Trail 2.4 miles. The trails are south of, and roughly between Lake Hart and Lake Mary Jane. Camping is allowed at Moss Park.

The area lies 10 miles south of Orlando and is split by the Orange/Osceola county line. CR-417 is a tollroad from I-4 that leads to CR-15. Take CR-15 south to Clap-Simms-Duda Road. Go east on that road 1.5 miles.

Managed by: Florida Fish and Wildlife Conservation Commission.

SPRING HAMMOCK PRESERVE/LAKE JESSUP SEGMENT, FLORIDA TRAIL
(Seminole County, 446 acres, hiking)

The Lake Jessup section of the Florida Trail passes through this park. Nearby Soldiers Park, another county park, provides some additional miles of hiking for those using the Florida Trail. From the west, the trail passes through this park, to Cross Seminole Trail and Oviedo, and on past Little Big Econ State Forest. From there it passes through Chuluota and into the Orlando Wetlands Park, before beginning its next segment in the Seminole Ranch Conservation Area. The Florida Trail northwest terminus is on US-17/92 south of Longwood 1 mile. The southeast terminus is at the entrance to the Seminole Ranch on Wheeler Road. From I-4, take CR-434 east to US-17/92, then go north to CR-419. The preserve stretches across CR-419. *Managed by: Seminole County.*

SPRUCE CREEK PRESERVE
(Volusia County, 2,000 acres, bicycling and hiking)

Over 7 miles of looping trails, including overlooks of Spruce Creek, wind in two loops, with connecting paths, through woods, hammock, and floodplain.

SR-44 is an exit of both I-4 and I-95. Going east from I-95, turn north on Sugar Mill. Turn west on Pioneer Trail. Turn east on Turnbull Bay Road and make the first left (north) on Martin Dairy Road, a dirt road. Martin Dairy makes a sharp leftward turn at the entrance to the preserve.

Managed by: Volusia County.

"THE SENATOR"
Big Tree Park adjoins Spring Hammock Preserve and is along the Lake Jessup Segment of the Florida Trail. In this park is "the Senator," a living cypress tree that may be 3,500 years old. Another cypress tree nearby is almost as old, although not as healthy in appearance. On weekends, a constant stream of visitors go to see the tree. It is mind-numbing to think that this tree existed before European Civilization and that it was 1,500 years old when Christ walked the earth.

Top: part of the Cassia Segment of the Florida Trail runs through Seminole State Forest.

STARKEY WILDERNESS PARK
(Pasco County, 7,870 acres, multi-use)

This former cattle ranch is now a well field and Florida's largest county park. Bike path: 3 miles. Hiking: 13. Equestrian: 10. Primary habitats: flatwoods, floodplain, and river. From I-75 or US-41, take SR-54 west toward New Port Richey, then north on Little Road, and east on River Crossing Boulevard to the entrance. The park is 15 miles west of Land O'Lakes. From US-19, go east from New Port Richey on SR-54 to Little Road. *Managed by: Pasco County.*

SUNCOAST PARKWAY TRAIL
(Citrus, Hernando, Hillsborough, and Pasco counties, bicycling and hiking)

From its conception, the Suncoast Parkway was controversial. It was opposed by environmental groups which felt both that this tollroad would open up much pristine land for development and would do too much damage to nature. Public concerns aside, the Parkway nears completion and is substantially open, allowing for rapid travel from western Hillsborough County to near Crystal River, an area served by only one other major highway, clogged US-19.

Besides the parkway is a 42- mile trail, some of it paved. The trail is restricted to bicycling and hiking, and early reports that equestrian use would be allowed have not proven so. Since the traffic is presently light, perhaps because of the tolls and lack of completion of the final leg, trail users will not be bothered by blaring horns. They will see a lot of gorgeous land when riding or walking this trail, but they best come prepared with sun block and water, for there is little shade except in the distance. From I-75 or

US-19, the trail can be accessed from SR-52 to the south and US-98 to the north. A parallel road to SR-52, Ridge Road, is the first access point. As of May 2001, the northern section of the Tollroad was not yet complete. *Managed by: Department of Transportation.*

TAMPA BYPASS CANAL
(Hillsborough County, bicycling and hiking)

Several hundred feet wide, the canal retains or diverts floodwaters from the Hillsborough River into McKay Bay. It stretches 14 miles from the Lower Hillsborough Flood Detention Area, meandering to the southwest. While its primary mission is flood control, the dikes on both sides provide wide bicycling, hiking, and jogging paths. In the summer, activity is best in early morning, as the sun can be brutal, and there is no shade. There is access at many places in Tampa including Trout Creek and the Lower Hillsborough Detention Area (behind the Big Top Flea Market on Fowler Avenue). A recreation guide, available from the water management district, details the access points. *Managed by: Southwest Florida Water Management District.*

TENOROC FISH MANAGEMENT AREA (TENOROC MINES)
(Polk County, 1,000 acres, multi-use)

A former phosphate mining area, Tenoroc is now largely devoted to large-mouth bass fishing in "lakes" which are former mining pits. The roads are open to bicycling and horse riding. There is a 6-mile hiking trail, built and maintained by volunteers. The terrain here is altered significantly as might be expected of a former

mining operation. From I-4 near Lakeland, take SR-33 at the easternmost exit, since there are two SR-33 exits. Proceed south to Tenoroc Mine Road, and take a left, proceeding to the headquarters, where it is necessry to register and pay a fee. *Managed by: Florida Fish and Wildlife Conservation Commission.*

Top: morning in the floodplain on part of the nature trail at Starkey Wilderness Park.
Bottom: crushed limerock road is part of the trail system in Starkey Wilderness Park.

THREE FORKS MARSH CONSERVATION AREA
(Brevard and Indian River counties, 52,000 acres, bicycling or hiking)

This area is essentially marsh with levees, or grassy dikes. In an open area like this, dike hiking or biking has many advantages, including easy walking or pedalling, and wide vistas. In fact, wildlife can be spotted quite some distance off with binoculars due to the open, flat nature of marsh. Water and sun block are important here. The area may be closed when restoration work is in progress. No horse riding is allowed. The trails are at Thomas Lawton Recreation Area, complete with picnic tables and portable toilets, at the absolute west end of CR-514, an exit of I-95. *Managed by: St. Johns River Water Management District.*

THREE LAKES WILDLIFE MANAGEMENT AREA
(Osceola County, 59,000+ acres, multi-use)

The three lakes are Jackson, Kissimmee, and Marian. The lakes are jewels around which are flatwoods, floodplain, hammock, marsh, prairie, and cypress swamps. This is a premier natural area, yet during the week, out of hunting season, there may be nobody around for miles.

Along the banks of Lake Jackson, whooping cranes are sometimes seen. This is where they were released as young juveniles. Two whooping crane chicks born in the wild in 2000 were the first to be born east of the Mississippi River in at least 60 years; one quickly perished from predators. This is sad, but normal, as whooper parents usually raise only one offspring at a time. In the end, both chicks perished.

A recent visitor to Prairie Lakes Unit reported that, in just a few minutes, deer, bobwhite, three types of hawks, turkeys, and a whooping crane were spotted. Red-cockaded woodpeckers and bald eagles are seen within the area also. This can all be enjoyed by bicycling on miles of roads, hiking over 60 miles, or using the 23 miles of blazed equestrian trail. The Florida Trail segment is 26.6 miles. Primitive camping is available by permit.

There are a number of prominent entrances. The entrance off SR-60 is west of US-441 perhaps 14 miles, and is a desolate place.

The Prairie Lakes Unit is a delight. It is located off CR-523 (Canoe Creek Road), and accessed by traveling either south from St. Cloud, west from US-441 at Kenansville, or north from Yeehaw Junction.

Just one-half mile southeast of the Prairie Lakes Unit entrance is a parking area and trailhead for a 1-mile loop nature trail, and a longer blazed trail stretching approximately 8 miles to the shores of Lake Marion.

Williams Road provides an entrance off US-441, 25 miles north of Yeehaw Junction.
Managed by: Florida Fish and Wildlife Conservation Commission.

TIGER CREEK PRESERVE
(Polk County, 4,580 acres, hiking)

Tiger Creek has a sand bottom and is fed by seepage. The preserve lies on both sides of Tiger Creek, south of Lake Kissimmee State Park,

and north of the Walk-in-the-Water Tract of Lake Wales Ridge State Forest. Habitats: flatwoods, marsh, river, scrub, and swamp.

For the eastern trailhead, go 6 miles east of Lake Wales on SR-60, then 4 miles south on Walk-in-the-Water Road, then turn west on Wakeford Road which dead-ends at the entrance. For the western trailhead on Pfundstein Road, turn east from SR-17 south of Hillcrest Heights onto Murray Road which ends at Pfundstein. There are two hiking trails off Pfundstein Road: a half-mile nature trail and 8.5 miles of Florida Trail. Equestrian trails are not part of the preserve, but a little further south of the western trailhead is the equestrian loop of the Walk-in-the-Water Tract.
Managed by: The Nature Conservancy.

TOSOHATCHEE STATE RESERVE
(Orange County, 34,000 acres, multi-use)

One reserve highlight is unspoiled Jim Creek Swamp, dominated by cypress, and a magnet for wildlife. Besides swamp, habitats include flatwoods, hardwood hammock, marsh, and river.

To the north of Tosohatchee, the Florida Trail enters and has a loop in the Seminole Ranch. Then it passes through Tosohatchee, including a loop, exiting through the Mormon Deseret Ranch. Overnight primitive camping is available at Tosohatchee with a permit. Through hikers on the Florida Trail do not need a permit and must exit the reserve through the front gate, and follow Taylor Creek Road to enter Deseret. There is one horse camp area, and those wishing to use it should call in advance. Bicycling is allowed on the generally firm roads. There are 27 miles of multi-use trails, and one 17-mile loop.

From the town of Christmas on SR-50, turn south on Taylor Creek Road. Go 3 miles to the entrance. Maps are available at the gate.

Top: along Jim Creek in Tosohatchee State Reserve.

THE CALL OF NATURE WHEN OUT IN NATURE
While many urban trails have tiled bathrooms, or at least portable toilets, many areas in wild, primitive condition do not. The etiquette when nature calls is to stay away from water sources, in part because long-distance hikers and those in emergency trouble may need to drink the water. One member of a group can carry a small shovel or trowel, and every backpack should have toilet paper.

TOWN AND COUNTRY GREENWAY TRAIL
(Hillsborough County)
See Upper Tampa Bay Trail

TRIPLE N RANCH WILDLIFE MANAGEMENT AREA
(Osceola County, 10,000+ acres, multi-use)

Triple N adjoins Bull Creek Wildlife Management Area. Perhaps 10 miles of multi-use trail (some sections dead-end) wind around it. Ecosystems: creeks, flatwoods, floodplain, lake, prairie, scrub, and swamp with cypress. Located west of I-95 approximately 30 miles, along US-192 east of Holopaw on the south side of the road. *Managed by: Florida Fish and Wildlife Conservation Commission.*

TROUT CREEK SITE
(Hillsborough County, bicycling and hiking).

There is a scenic, short boardwalk and equally short nature trails. However, this little park, full of palmettos dominated by pine or oak, grants access to the dikes of the Tampa Bypass Canal, and the beginning of a 15-mile loop connecting it to Flatwoods Park and Morris Bridge. From I-75, exit onto Fletcher Avenue east which becomes Morris Bridge Road. The entrance appears almost immediately on the north side of the road. *Managed by: Southwest Florida Water Management District.*

ULUMAY WILDLIFE SANCTUARY
(Brevard County, 457 acres, bicycling and hiking)

Along the Indian River Lagoon, there are 8 miles of packed dikes for biking and hiking. The area is a terrific canoe and kayak opportunity. Ecosystems: floodplain, marsh, and river. On Merritt Island, from the Beeline (CR-528) turn south on Banana River Drive and west on Audubon Road. *Managed by: Brevard County.*

UPPER HILLSBOROUGH TRACT
(Hillsborough and Pasco counties, 6,225 acres, multi-use)

The tract is cut roughly in two by CR-54. The larger and gated portion is to the south, where there are firm, multi-use roads. The northern portion has enough sand in places to stop a tank. Camping, equestrian use, and equestrian camping require permits. There are perhaps 5 miles of loop roads in the southern section, and about 3 in the northern portion. A 5-mile trail is maintained by the Florida Trail Association.

This area is one headwater of the historic Green Swamp and is a natural retention area of the Hillsborough River. The river meanders through it in normal times, but it is dry floodplain during drought. The natural habitats are flatwoods and floodplain, with both slash and longleaf pine.

From I-75, proceed east on SR-54 into Zephyrhills. SR-54 stops at US-301. Turn north on US-301, then shortly turn east on CR-54. US-98 crosses CR-54 east of the Tract. The bike and equestrian trailhead is between Zephyrhills and US-98 just west of railroad tracks. The

hiking trailhead is on the west side of CR-535, across from the airport. Go east on CR-54, then turn south on CR-535.

Managed by: Southwest Water Management District.

UPPER TAMPA BAY TRAIL
(Hillsborough County, bicycling and hiking)

This trail has also been identified as the Upper Hillsborough Trail. It combines with the Town and Country Greenway Trail for 3 miles each way. Plans exist to greatly expand this trail so that it runs from Rocky Point in the vicinity of Tampa International Airport to Lutz Lake Fern Road near Lutz, where it will extend to the Suncoast Trail. At present it is open only for bicycling and foot traffic, but equestrian use is planned.

In Tampa, the trail is west of Dale Mabry Highway, a north-south road that intersects I-275 and passes by Buccaneer Stadium. From Dale Mabry, Hillsborough Avenue leads to the current southern trailheads on Hanley (Shimberg Park) and Webb roads. Other trailheads are at Wilsky Road and Gunn Highway. Consulting a city street map is helpful for the out of town visitor, as the trailheads are not on major highways. Visit or call the Ranger Station at 7508 Ehrlich Road. The phone number is 813-264-8512.

Top: a view from a bridge on the Van Fleet Trail.

VAN FLEET STATE TRAIL
(Lake, Sumter, and Polk counties, multi-use)

The 29+ miles of this rail-to-trail shoot right through the heart of the Green Swamp. Like most railway trails, it seems straight without deviation. The railroad was originally built by Henry Plant to move phosphate.

Even in cold weather, many reptiles can be seen in the creeks, marsh, and swamp along the trail. A small selection includes alligators, gopher tortoise, mud turtles, pygmy rattlesnakes, and ribbon snakes. During a recent visit, an exceptionally large otter climbed over the road from one pond to another. In addition to the wetlands, other habitats beside the trail include flatwoods, hardwood hammocks, and prairie. There is a parallel equestrian trail.

Northern terminus: 20 miles east of I-75 on the south side of SR-50, near Mabel. Southern terminus: on SR-33, west of Polk City 2 miles, and on the north side of the road.

PAP

WEEDEN ISLAND PRESERVE
(Pinellas County, 1,300 acres, hiking)

There are two trails for hiking and nature observation: Boy Scout Trail is 1 mile round trip, while Getting Trail is approximately 3 miles. Getting Trail includes two boardwalks through mangroves, overlooks of two estuary "lakes," and an observation tower. Birding is terrific in this preserve.

On Weeden Island there are Timucuan burial grounds. They are currently on Florida Power property, but there are negotiations to build a boardwalk, then join the preserve with the nearby Friendship Trail over the old Gandy Bridge and Tampa Bay.

Timucuans were Florida Native Americans who predated the arrival of the Europeans. It was a common practice of these early Americans to bury their dead in mounds, the bodies eviscerated, with different parts buried in different mounds. The mounds at Weeden were such burial mounds. Weeden Island is listed in the National Registry of Historic Sites.

Bicycles are allowed on the main park road, and just about anywhere but the boardwalk. There is a 4-mile canoe trail. The waters around Weeden Island are an aquatic preserve protecting the sea grass beds.

In St. Petersburg, from Gandy Boulevard (US-92), go south on San Martin Boulevard 1 mile. The county park is on Weeden Island Drive. *Managed by: Pinellas County.*

WEEKIWACHEE PRESERVE
(Hernando County, 7,000 acres, bicycling and hiking)

This preserve includes altered land with mining pits containing sky-blue water, as well as freshwater marsh and hammock. From the entrance given below, the trail in is about 1 mile. To the north is a loop of 4.3 miles, and to the south is a trail of almost 3 miles to an alternate gate. From Weeki Wachee on US-19, go west on CR-550 to CR-597/595, then turn south. The trailhead is approximately 1 mile south of the county park. CR-597/595 passes by some scenic saltmarsh on the Gulf side, with hammock islands in the distance. *Managed by: Southwest Florida Water Management District.*

WEKIVA RIVER CONSERVATION AREA
(Seminole County, 2,340 acres, bicycling and hiking)

Formerly designated as the Wekiva River Buffer, this area is essentially floodplain between the Wekiva and Little Wekiva rivers, with cypress along the water, and hardwoods and palms set among palmettos. The trail is 1.5 miles in, 1.5 miles out.

It is said that this land forms a corridor for black bear, yet the trailhead is in a very large housing development, complete with golf course, a beautiful pond with fountain, luxury homes, and apartments. It is hard to imagine Florida's shy, elusive black bear roaming so close to the sound of humming air-conditioners, the *tsk-tsk-tsk* of sprinklers, and the other sounds of suburbia. However, bears and many other wild animals better adjusted to human presence are seen on the trail.

The trail receives considerable use from local residents who jog, walk, and ride their bicycles on it. It is not worth a trip from Nebraska, but it can be combined with visits to Lower Wekiva River State Preserve, Rock Springs Run State Preserve, Seminole State Forest, and Wekiwa Springs State Park.

From I-4, northeast of Orlando, go west on SR-434, to Wekiva Springs Road. Go through the Sable Point Development on the north side of the road to Wilderness Drive.

Managed by: St. Johns River Water Management District.

Top: **scenic saltmarsh along coastal roads near Weekiwatchee Preserve.**

WEKIWA SPRINGS STATE PARK
(Orange and Seminole counties, 8,135 acres, multi-use)

Diversity and beauty are the outstanding features of Wekiwa. It has flatwoods, floodplain, hardwood hammocks, lakes, sandhill, scrub, springs, swamp, and river, all close together, with often abrupt transitions. It is an ideal spot for budding naturalists to learn habitat identification and recognize transition zones.

It is also a wonderful place for recreation. With nearby Lower Wekiva State Preserve and Rock Springs Run State Reserve, there is plenty of bicycling, camping, canoeing, hiking, horseback riding, and swimming. It is a good idea, especially if it is not just a day visit, to coordinate with all three public lands offices to find out current conditions and availability. There are 13.5 miles of trails in Wekiwa, with approximately 8 miles for equestrian use. It is a popular place to canoe, with rentals within the park (and outside of it run by private outfitters).

Bicyclists will be delighted with the 3 miles of service road, 2.5 miles of paved bike trail, and 5 miles of off-road trail.

The park is named for the Wekiva River. According to many linguists, that spelling and the spelling Wekiwa are likely the same Native American word, just pronounced and written differently, although some people believe that they have two different meanings. Even park officials confuse the two at times.

From I-4 at Longwood, go west on CR-434 for 1 mile. Turn north on Wekiva Springs Road and follow the signs.

Top: along the trail in River Camp in Wekiwa Springs State Park.

Middle: a deer in dawn fog at Wekiwa Springs State Park.

Below, right: early morning along the Sandhill Trail in Lower Wekiva State Preserve.

PC

WITHLACOOCHEE RIVER PARK
(Pasco County, 400 acres, hiking)

A great deal of effort has gone into constructing 4.5 miles of scenic trails and several boardwalks which pass through flatwoods, floodplain, and marsh, and along the Withlacoochee River. There is a sturdy observation tower. The park adjoins the Green Swamp West Trail, a 21 mile trail maintained by the Florida Trail Association. Thus, it is possible from here to embark on a considerable foot journey. From US-301 in Dade City, go east 3 miles on River Road, then south a short distance on Anton Road to the entrance.
Managed by: Pasco County.

WITHLACOOCHEE STATE FOREST
(Citrus, Hernando, Pasco, and Sumter counties, 150,000+ acres, multi-use)

This forest has four separate major areas or tracts (Citrus, Croom, Jumper Creek, and Richloam), and two separate smaller ones (Colonel Robbins and McKethan). While the smaller areas each have short nature trails, the larger ones have substantial trails, and are generally open to multi-use.

Bicycling. The Southwest Association of Mountain Bike Pedallers (the SWAMP Club) has built a mountain bike trail in Croom, and bicycling is allowed on all roads and trails, except the Florida Trail segments. There are 60 total miles of bicycling within the forest. The Withlacoochee State Trail can be accessed from several points within the forest and is 46 miles (one way) with a parallel equestrian path.

Equestrian. Citrus has 46 miles of horse trails and overnight stabling. There are also equestrian trails in Croom. The stable can be reached at 352-344-4238.

Hiking. Florida Trail Association volunteers maintain trails in three tracts: Citrus (40 miles), Croom (22 miles), and Richloam (31.5 miles). The Richloam Tract has some exceptional bridges built by volunteers. There are three other long trails: Hog Island (6.8 miles), Colonel Robbins (2.5 miles), and McKethan Lake (2.5 miles).

Jumper Creek has roads and trails in a very primitive state. Trailhead locations, maps, and brochures can be requested in advance.

The forest is a popular camping area, with many options, and a popular swimming spot.

Named for the Withlacoochee River, there are also quality canoe and kayak adventures here. Some are on Silver Lake, most are on the river. Florida has two Withlacoochee Rivers, and this one is sometimes referred to as the Withlacoochee South. It is along this river where Osceola lived and fought US government forces during the Seminole Wars from what is called the Cove of the Withlacoochee.

At the Brooksville exit on I-75, go east on SR-50 for Croom and Richloam. Citrus is west of CR-581, southwest of Inverness. Jumper Creek is reached by exiting west on CR-470 from I-75, and going 2 miles toward Lake Panasoffkee, then turning left on CR-479. Turn right after 1 mile on CR-416, and follow the signs.

WEST ORANGE RAIL TRAIL
(Orange County, bicycling and hiking)

This rail-to-trail has been greatly expanded and is now a 19-mile trail through Winter Garden from Apopka to Oakland. There are plans to add even more distance to it. There are eight trailheads along the way. Mile 19 is located along CR-424 to the west of the Orange Blossom Trail (US-441), a very heavily used intersection. Mile zero is at the County Line Station off SR-50 near Oakland. *Managed by: Orange County.*

WILDERNESS PARK/MORRIS BRIDGE PARK
(Hillsborough County, 7,223 acres, bicycling and hiking)

This trail includes a 3-mile round trip on an old railroad tram to an overlook of the Hillsborough River. Several things are appealing to those in search of great views: the canopy over the road near the river, the walk along the primitive trail among the cypress knees, a

Above: a bicyclist passes a hiker in Morris Bridge Park. The bicylist will soon approach a gazebo by the Hillsborough River where she can rest for the return trip.

circular boardwalk through floodplain, and the river itself. (Cypress knees are thought to serve two purposes: they may stabilize the tree and help it to breathe.)

This unit is connected by bike paths to the Morris Bridge Bicycle Area, Trout Creek Site to the west, and Flatwoods Park to the northeast. It is part of the Wilderness Park Off-Road Trails, which are very popular with bicyclists.

From I-75, exit east on Fletcher Avenue which becomes Morris Bridge Road. Go 5 miles to the entrance just before the bridge over the Hillsborough River. There are parking lots on both sides of the road, but sometimes the lot on the south side is locked.
Managed by: Southwest Florida Water Management District.

PC

WITHLACOOCHEE STATE TRAIL
(Citrus, Hernando, Marion, and Sumter counties, multi-use)

This 46-mile rail-to-trail begins in Dunellon, parallels the Withlacoochee River, and extends through sections of the Withlacoochee State Forest, as well as through towns. There are many entry points along the way, including some in the forest. An equestrian trail is adjacent to the paved path. A map is available that shows all trailheads (see Appendix for address). Northern terminus: off US-41 south of Dunellon. Southern: south of Trilby on US-301/98.

WITHLACOOCHEE
Three important areas for recreation in this region bear the name Withlacoochee: Withlacoochee River Park, Withlacoochee State Foest, and Withlacoochee State Trail. All are named for the southern Withlacoochee River. There is also a river of the same name in North Florida that is a tributary of the Suwannee. In the Creek language, spoken by Florida's Seminoles, the word means "little big water."

Top: two riders cross over SR-50 on a concrete bridge along the Withlacoochee State Trail.

THE WITHLACOOCHEE CAVERNS
Even experienced forest visitors are generally unaware that Withlacoochee State Forest has caves which can be explored in Citrus County. Narrow, twisty, and claustrophobic, they require an experienced guide for safety. Some of the caves have interesting names: Danger, Peace, Potty, Sick Bat, and Vandal.

SHORTER CENTRAL FLORIDA TRAILS

CARLTON RESERVE
(Sarasota County)

There is a nature trail in a series of loops through flatwoods, hammocks, marsh, and swamp. From I-75, south of Sarasota and east of Venice, go east on Jacaranda Road. It quickly comes to a dead-end. Then, turn south on the paved road and follow the prominent signs.

LAKE MANATEE STATE RECREATION AREA
(Manatee County)

This popular boating, camping, and fishing site has a number of short trails, which combined total 2.8 miles for hiking or horse riding. Habitats: flatwoods, lake, and scrub dominated by sand pine. Go east from I-75 on SR-64 for 8 miles.

LETTUCE LAKE PARK
(Hillsborough County)

This small county park on the edge of the Hillsborough River has a paved loop of 1.4 miles, a 3500-foot boardwalk along the Hillsborough River, and a number of short trails through the flatwoods. Habitats: flatwoods, floodplain, river, and swamp. From I-75, go west a short distance on Fletcher Avenue in Tampa. The entrance is on the north side of the road.

RYE WILDERNESS PARK
(Manatee County)

The relatively short hiking trails in this county park are redeemed by overlooks of the Little Manatee River. Equestrian trails can also be hiked. From I-75, go 2 miles east on SR-64, then north on Rye Road to the park. Prominent signs are posted along the way.

SOUTH FORK OF THE ST. LUCIE TRAIL
(Martin County)

This 1-mile trail on South Florida Water Management District Land is maintained by Florida Trail volunteers. It is alongside the South Fork of the St. Lucie River and is accessible only from the river. The river can be accessed from Hosford Park. From I-95, turn onto SR-76 and go east to Cove Road.

TURKEY CREEK SANCTUARY
(Brevard County)

A 1.25-mile boardwalk, a 0.75-mile jogging path, and a 0.9-mile loop through hammock combine for something just short of 3 miles. There is also scrub habitat above the creek including sand pine. From I-95, exit east on Palm Bay Road, then south on Babcock Street, and go east on Port Malabar Boulevard. It is less then 2 miles to the entrance.

PC

Above: roller blading couple on the paved path at Lettuce Lake, a county park in Tampa. The park has this 1.4-mile paved path, and short nature trails through flatwoods.

Opposite page: mangroves in fog.

RS-SI

South Florida offers the sights and views most unique to the state. It certainly isn't Kansas. Sometimes, if your mind drifts while driving north Florida highways, you might wonder if you are in Alabama or Georgia, but this does not happen in South Florida. The Big Cypress, Everglades, the Keys, and Lake Okeechobee are distinctly Florida, and they inspire not merely cross-continental trips, but draw international visitors.

Much of the area historically was an extension of the overflow from Lake Okeechobee. Until the construction of the Hoover Dike, the water overflowed from it, in a manner often described as sheet flow, and moved slowly down a slight incline to feed the Everglades. Nowadays an enormous portion of the Florida Trail circles the lake on more than 100 miles of this dike.

A great diversity of trees and plants is found in the region because South Florida is located between temperate and tropical weather zones. Thus many plants, vines, and trees that could not survive northward thrive there, including orchids and bromeliads in natural profusion, and tropical trees, such as Jamaica dogwood, wild tamarind, mastic, Geiger tree, gumbo limbo, and mahogany.

There are many smaller recreational trails within the region, some of them quite splendid. Compared to the enormity of the Big Cypress and Everglades, however, they all seem diminished. One exception to this is Fakahatchee Strand State Preserve. The "Fak" is a very special place with an astonishingly rich fauna and flora, and a few of the remaining Florida panthers.

South Florida's typical sights include an abundance of alligators. They are seen along many road and waterways, and floating in ponds

Above: **bicyclists riding on the beach at Sanibel Island on a windy day.**

Opposite page: **orange milkweed along the shore at Babcock-Webb Wildlife Management Area north of Ft. Myers.**

and canals. Perhaps the bird most associated with the region's current condition is the snail kite, or Everglade kite, since it is dependent on an abundance of apple snails in the Everglades for continued existence. Another is the endangered Cape Sable seaside sparrow.

The Florida panther, perhaps the most powerful symbol of vanishing Florida, is found mostly in South Florida, and usually no further north than some of the Central Region. Panther sightings are exceptionally rare, but trail users are likely to be full of hope, and perhaps that optimism might be rewarded with a once-in-a-lifetime sighting.

BABCOCK-WEBB WILDLIFE MANAGEMENT AREA

(Charlotte County, 69,000+ acres, bicycling and hiking)

On some maps, this is incorrectly called the C. M. Webb Wildlife Management Area.

The imminent addition of trails here may be very significant. Neighboring Lee County's seven regional parks are not even 1/10th the size. Until the recreational trails are added, there are 5 miles one way of paved road that makes for excellent bicycle rides. There are also packed and soft sand roads, and foot paths. Primitive camping is allowed with permit.

A few endangered red-cockaded woodpeckers make their homes within the area. Alligators are prominent in the popular fishing lake. This is a big enough, faraway place that almost any wild animal found in South Florida could show up here. The habitats include flatwoods, marsh, ponds, and lakes.

Exit I-75 north of Ft. Myers and south of Port Charlotte at the Tropical Acres exit. Go east about 1 mile to the check station.

Managed by: Florida Fish and Wildlife Conservation Commission.

PC

BAHIA HONDA STATE PARK
(Monroe County, 524 acres, hiking).

While there is a short nature trail (0.5 mile), the greatest joy is found along the 2.8 miles of beach. On US-1, 12 miles south of Marathon, in the Keys.

BIG CYPRESS NATIONAL PRESERVE
(Collier and Hendry counties, 730,000+ acres, multi-use)

This preserve is indeed extensive, hence "big." The predominant tree is cypress, both pond and bald cypress. The Big Cypress is probably the closest thing left to what South Florida was like before humans arrived.

In addition to the cypress swamps, there are hardwood hammocks, extensive marshes, prairie, saltmarsh, and bays and mangroves in the coastal areas. There is plentiful wildlife by day and night - alligators, deer, otters, and raccoons are conspicuous. Many smaller creatures are less obvious, but equally abundant and fascinating.

On the preserve are members of the remaining Florida panther population. They are occasionally seen crossing the roads or running through grass. While some believe the Florida panther population may have "turned the corner," as it reportedly now approaches 100, others are more skeptical. The panther suffers from the continued dwindling of natural habitat, and the pace of development in Collier and Lee counties does not bode well for the survival of Florida's cougar.

Another large mammal - bear - can be found here. The South Florida population of bear is considered threatened.

During the winter migratory season, birding is exceptional throughout the area.

Loop Road, running from US-41 at Monroe Station south and then east to Fortymile Bend, is a 26-mile, often pothole-filled drive for vehicles, popular with cyclists. This road passes ponds which are a favorite habitat of otters.

A 33.5-mile portion of the Florida Trail stretches from the rest area on I-75, across US-41, to Loop Road. Conditions vary, and it is best to check with the headquarters before proceeding.

The 21.5-mile Big Cypress Seminole Segment of the Florida Trail is along levees L-2 and L-3, by farms, and through lands owned by US Sugar Corporation. It also passes by the Seminole Tribe's Billie Swamp Safari and the Ak-Tha-Thi-Ki Museum. At present, usage is limited to eight hikers per month, fine in summer, but insufficient in winter. The Florida Trail Association is hoping to negotiate increased usage.

Some of the northern roads in the Big Cypress also pass through marsh, and in the rainy season it is not unusual to see bicyclists walking through a waist-deep portion of the road with their bicycle held over their head. This is particularly true at Bear Island. Camping and primitive camping are available, but check with the headquarters located on US-41 approximately 16 miles to the east of SR-29. Maps and directions can be obtained at the headquarters where the staff is exceptionally helpful.

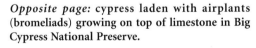

Opposite page: cypress laden with airplants (bromeliads) growing on top of limestone in Big Cypress National Preserve.

Top, left: a volunteer blazing a portion of the Florida Trail segment in Big Cypress National Preserve. There are two Florida Trail segments within the Big Cypress.

Top, right: determined backpackers hiking a section of the Florida Trail in Big Cypress National Preserve. While trail flooding is heaviest in the summer rainy season, a portion of the trail is always wet.

Middle, left: exposed limestone along the Florida Trail in Big Cypress National Preserve. This type of habitat is referred to as South Florida rockland.

Below, right: a hiker pauses to study an airplant in bloom in the Big Cypress National Preserve.

MS-SI

BISCAYNE NATIONAL PARK
(Dade County, 173,000 acres, hiking)

Most of Biscayne's adventures are aquatic, and the typical visitor comes here to dive. There are splendid reefs, and 37 barrier islands. Glass bottom and dive boats go to the reefs, and kayaks and canoes can be rented to paddle through the waters and around the mangroves.

There is a hiking trail on Elliott Key 7 miles long. Between May and October mosquitoes on the barrier island can be brutal. There is no regular boat service to the island, however, many nearby marinas offer boat rentals. Camping is available on Elliott and Boca Chita Keys and reservations for boat transportation can be made though the park's concession.

From US-1 in Homestead, take SW 320th Street east to the park headquarters at Convoy Point.

CALOOSAHATCHEE REGIONAL PARK
(Lee County, 800 acres, multi-use)

It is obvious that a great deal of quality effort has gone into making this park. On the south side of River Road, it is along the banks of the Caloosahatchee River where there are palms and oaks, with vines and ferns, in dense hammock. There is a quick transition into pine flatwoods, and two short hiking trails of 1.3 and 2.3 miles.

On the north side of the road are bicycle and equestrian trails totaling over 10 miles on which hikers are encountered.

Lee County has a number of recreational areas, but this one is the largest and best organized. The park also leads occssional trips on Hickey Creek, a state-designated canoe trail, which runs into the Caloosahatchee River. A new recreational area was scheduled in the Hickey Creek area with 6 miles of hiking, but some problems have delayed this.

From I-75, take the North Ft. Myers exit, go east on SR-78 about 4 miles to the stop sign, then 1 mile north on SR-31, turning east at River Road, and proceeding 7 miles.

Managed by: Lee County.

CAPE HAZE PIONEER TRAIL
(Charlotte County)

This paved rail-to-trail is almost 4 miles one way. There are plans to connect it to the bicycle trail on Gasparilla Island. When completed, that will make a spectacular journey. From US-41 in Port Charlotte, turn west on SR-776 and proceed to Charlotte Beach. The trailhead is south of the intersection of SR-776 and CR-771. *Managed by: Charlotte County.*

(BILL BAGGS) CAPE FLORIDA STATE RECREATION AREA
(Dade County, 567 acres, bicycling and hiking).

Located on Key Biscayne, there are almost 4 miles of shoreline, 0.5 miles of paved road, and a 1.2-mile paved path. This is a busy facility, with bathouses, boardwalks, and fishing piers, in addition to a lighthouse. From US-1, take the Rickenbacker Causeway east.

Top: **a father tows his snorkeling children through the clear water at Biscayne National Park.**

From I-95 in West Palm Beach, go west on Forest Hill Boulevard in West Palm Beach for 5 miles. The entrance is on the south side of the road, but it will be necessary to park on the north side in Okeeheelee Park.

Managed by: Palm Beach County.

COLLIER-SEMINOLE STATE PARK
(Collier County, 6,425 acres, bicycling and hiking)

The park includes saltmarsh and mangroves, marking the north reach of Florida's Ten Thousand Islands. It contains a nature trail with a boardwalk that is almost a mile long, and a 3-mile mountain bike trail open to hiking. Bicyclists should check in at the park entrance and obtain a key to use the gated trail.

The 6.5-mile Florida Trail Loop is located across US-41 from the park entrance and passes near a Miccosukee village in the western portion. The Miccosukee are Seminoles who split from the Seminole Tribe of Florida over political differences. Hikers should not enter the village and should respect the privacy of the Miccosukee, just as they would like privacy if the trail passed by their homes. Sometimes the Florida Trail Loop is closed because the trail has not been cleared recently, is overly wet, or because of terrible concentrations of mosquitoes. Thus, those desiring to hike this section should check in advance with the park, or come to enjoy the other wonderful trails and activities, and hope it is open.

For off-land adventures, there is a concession boat tour of the mangroves, and this is a popular kayak area, but checking with rangers concerning float plans is required, and an exceptionally good safety measure. The park is also a popular campground.

Since this area borders on the tropical weather zone, where freezes rarely occur, it has Caribbean trees, such as the copper-colored gumbo limbo. One prominent South Florida habitat not found farther northward is the tropical hardwood hammock, an area of higher ground where tropical hardwood trees prosper.

Located 18 miles south of Naples on US-41.

CAYO COSTA STATE PARK
(In the Gulf of Mexico off Lee County, 2,100 acres, bicycling and hiking)

This beautiful barrier island has mangroves on the mainland side and a pristine beach on the Gulf. One of the joys of coming here is discovering what Sanibel and Captiva were like before development.

Between the dock and the beach is almost 1 mile of road, traveled by foot or tram. There are three north-south trails of 5.5 total miles: dockside is Quarantine Trail; halfway to the beach, Cemetery Trail; and near the beach, Gulf Trail. These trails are crossed and interwoven east-west by the Scrub Trail and the Pinewood Trail. The pristine beach provides several additional miles for strolls. All trails are open to bicyclists and hikers. Visitors must bring their own bikes. Kayaks can journey to and from many of the adjoining islands.

There is a concession in Bokeelia on Pine Island that transports those without boats. Cabins are available on the island. To reach Bokeelia, take Pine Island Road west from US-41 in North Ft. Myers. Pine Island Road is the North Ft. Myers exit of I-75. From US-41, go 13 miles west, and then turn north on Stringfellow Road. Follow it to the tip of the island. The concession has changed in the past, so it is best to inquire in advance.

CHOLEE PARK
(Palm Beach County, 800 acres, bicycling and hiking)

This recreation area may trouble some. The 5-mile trail is mostly through melaleuca. This exotic "punk" tree has done much harm to the Florida environment. It has the benefit, however, of being relatively soft if you crash while riding a bicycle (or if you fall on it).

One of the problems with melaleuca, other than choking out native plants, is that it evapotranspires a lot of water. During drought times, Florida can have water shortages. Another problem is that it is difficult to eradicate, although expensive eradication programs are underway as can be witnessed on many highways, including I-75 south of Ft. Myers.

Cholee has been closed for construction and was not open as of publication date.

Top, left: along the shoreline at Cayo Costa State Park.
Top, right: a colorful portion of the trunk of a royal palm at Collier-Seminole State Park.

(J. W.) CORBETT WILDLIFE MANAGEMENT AREA
(Palm Beach County, 60,225 acres, multi-use)

The 14 (usually lonely) miles of the Florida Trail in Corbett begin at the Everglades Youth Conservation Camp, reached by a connector from Dupuis Reserve. Although the trail is one way, and must be retraced, making the hike 28 miles, a second car may be parked at various points in and out of Corbett or Dupuis to shorten the trip. The trail is primarily through marsh with flatwoods. Bring a compass, a map, and a friend. Primitive overnight camping is available to hikers. In addition, there is the approximately 1-mile, scenic Hungryland Boardwalk in the woods and around a cypress swamp. There are many multi-use miles of graded, paved, and shell road.

Top, left: a portion of Hungryland Boardwalk in Corbett Wildlife Management Area.
Top, right: balloon vine growing in South Florida.

There are two entrances. The North Gate is 8 miles to the east of Indiantown on the south side of SR-71. It is usually locked. For the south entrance, continue south on SR-710, and turn west on Northlake Boulevard. There are prominent signs until you pass the regional office of the Florida Fish and Wildlife Conservation Commission. Then there are no signs, making a visitor wonder if something has been missed. But, it has not. Continue to the end of Northlake Boulevard and turn north on Seminole Pratt Whitney Road. This road leads into Corbett, where the Everglades Youth Camp and one Florida Trail trailhead are located.

Managed by: Florida Fish and Wildlife Conservation Commission.

THE BIG ITCH

Those who wish to avoid Florida's biting bugs might limit outdoor adventures to the period from mid-September to the end of April. Those are cooler months, particularly in northern Florida. The worrisome insects are mosquitoes, biting flies (especially horse and yellow flies), and "no-see-ums," or sand flies. While mosquitoes show up in many wet areas, they can be a plague in mangroves, South Florida, and the Keys. The biting flies have shorter seasons, in spring to summer. There are rare cases of mosquito-born encephalitis in Florida.

Tick and chigger (redbug) bites can also cause great discomfort, probably more intense than biting flies, and longer-lasting. Both are arachnids, relatives of spiders, with six legs at birth, and eight as adults.

Contrary to popular belief, chiggers do not bury larvae in the skin. Rather, they bite much like a mosquito, and the first bite is to find out if they are biting a reptile. If not, they climb off. While chiggers in the Old World do carry disease, Florida chiggers only harbor interminable itching.

Florida ticks do on occasion carry diseases. The most notorious, Lyme's disease, does not occur in Florida, according to entomologists, although there are enough popular reports to be cautious. The second most dangerous, Rocky Mountain spotted fever, does occur, but only rarely. A person who becomes sick within a few days of a woods visit should check with a doctor. Florida ticks can cause a flu-like disease called ehrlichiosis.

Scientists have evaluated all the folk remedies for ticks and it seems they only make matters worse. An embedded tick should be removed in a slow, steady pull. It is wise to apply antiseptic.

Perhaps the best all around weapon for Florida's biting things is repellent with DEET. However, many would rather put up with the bugs than spray their skin with a substance that is known to dissolve plastic.

CREW MANAGEMENT AREA/ CORKSCREW MARSH

(Lee County, 7,140 acres, bicycling and hiking)

Recreational activities center on 5 miles of mowed hiking paths. This is mostly flatwoods, some marsh, with a 12-foot observation tower overlooking a seasonal pond. From I-75 near Naples, take Corkscrew Road east (this is not the road to Corkscrew Swamp Sanctuary). Seventeen miles east from the interstate, the entrance is on the south side of the road. *Managed by: South Florida Water Management District.*

Top: looking out over Corkscrew Marsh in Crew Management Area.
Above, left: the observation platform at Corkscrew Marsh.

Above, right: a trail through flatwoods in Crew Management Area.

DING DARLING NATIONAL WILDLIFE REFUGE

(Lee County, 6,355 acres, bicycling and hiking)

Ding Darling is named for the famous cartoonist, and creator of the Duck Stamp. It is a wonderful place for observing migratory and resident birds, as well as other resident wildlife. For birders, Ding Darling is fabled. The refuge is vigorously supported by local residents, many of whom volunteer their time and efforts.

This is primarily mangrove and bay estuary, with dikes originally built for mosquito control. An estuary system is especially rich in marine life, and Ding Darling's has many fish, including mullet, red and mangrove snapper, and redfish.

Trails: Bailey Trail, 1.75 mile. Shell road for autos, bicyclists, hikers: 4 miles, one way. Shell Mound Trail: 0.33-mile hiking trail. Sanibel Island Bike Paths: 26 miles, one way, outside the refuge. Indigo Hiking Trail: 2 miles one way, 4 round trip.

Reaching Ding Darling during peak tourist seasons may entail a lengthy delay on two roads: the causeway to Sanibel, and the drive north on Sanibel-Captiva Road to Wildlife Drive. The time along the causeway seems hardly wasted because of the beauty of the water, renowned for its Caribbean colors. Patience along Sanibel-Captiva will be rewarded once at Ding Darling.

Exit I-75 in Ft. Myers on Daniels Parkway, turn southwest onto Six Mile Cypress, cross US-41, and keep going until crossing the Sanibel Island Toll Bridge and coming to a stop sign. Turn north on Periwinkle and follow the signs. It is a half-hour drive or more from the interstate. Maps are available at the refuge headquarters.

Top: a large congregation of white pelicans on Marco Island.

Above: a roseate spoonbill about to take flight. This beautiful species is easily observed at Ding Darling.

Top: a waterspout in the Gulf of Mexico.
---All the following are at Ding Darling---
Middle, left: many wading birds congregating.
Middle, right: white ibis gobbling up a fiddler crab.
Bottom, left: white ibis standing on the Indigo Trail.
Bottom, right: a large alligator walking.

DUPUIS RESERVE
(Martin and Palm Beach counties, 21,875 acres, multi-use)

This is a large, isolated area, where a compass, map, and a companion are very good precautions, whether on horseback or foot. It has one of the few long equestrian trails in South Florida–17.5 miles.

There are over 35 miles of the Florida Trail composed of four loops ranging from 5 to 15.6 miles. This includes a 7-mile connector into adjacent Corbett Wildlife Management Area.

Although bicycles can be ridden on two roads for 7 miles, these can be difficult, especially when wet. Even vehicles might find the going slippery.

Overnight camping is available at four designated locations: the equestrian center for equestrian users, a family campground, a group campground, and a remote campsite. Contact the water management district concerning camping.

Major habitats: flatwoods, small lakes, marsh, with some swamp, and scrub.

There are trailheads on the south side of SR-76, about 3 miles east of Lake Okeechobee and Port Mayaca.

Managed by: South Florida Water Management District.

Above: **bicyclist atop a mound at Dyer Park.**

DYER PARK
(Palm Beach County, 405 acres, multi-use)

Dyer has three trails of roughly equal length totaling nearly 10 miles. Two are bicycle trails and one is equestrian. Dyer provides many recreational opportunities, and is heavily used, but in some sense it is a spectacle. It is built over a former landfill, and it has large hills that are former garbage heaps. One hill is sufficiently steep that it has stopped many a cyclist lacking a good head start, despite down-shifting gears. This is perhaps the only mountain in flat South Florida to mountain bike. Located just off SR-710 in the community of Dyer, near the junction of SR-710 and Military Trail (SR-809).

Managed by: Palm Beach County.

EVERGLADES NATIONAL PARK
(Collier, Dade, and Monroe counties, 1,500,000+ acres, multi-use)

Those who are unfamiliar with the Everglades think of it as some kind of jungle. As an ecosystem, however, jungle is non-existent in Florida.

What you do see in the Glades is astounding. The central marsh looks like prairie–flat, almost treeless, and seemingly endless. Unlike other large wetlands, these waters historically began as the overflow of a lake, Lake Okeechobee, and not from river flooding, making the Everglades unique in the world. This uniqueness is one reason it is a national treasure. It is also a life source for birds and other animals, whose numbers plummeted sharply last century when humans changed the Everglades permanently.

At its heart is a vast basin marsh, with a slow, gradual sheet flow of water over a very slight decline to the sea. In it are tree islands, or small hammocks, and "gator holes," alligator wallows where water remains and life continues in the dry season.

The dominant plant is sawgrass, and beneath it on the marsh bottom lies periphyton, a collection of algae–food for small fish. Around the Everglades' coastal edges are mangroves. The Ten Thousand Islands are to the west, and Florida Bay is to the south. At the roots of mangroves, mud and leaf detritus accumulate, and this may result eventually in the formation of island-like thickets where many birds feed, and various marine organisms prosper.

The general public can enter Everglades National Park at two locations. Shark Valley is 30 miles west of Miami on US-41, and has a paved 15-mile bicycle and walking path to a large tower where the Everglades vastness (and some very large alligators) can be observed easily. There is a tram ride to and from the tower for those who prefer not to walk or bike.

SR-9336 has an entrance that is the gateway to many trails, both long and short for bicycling and hiking, as well as canoe trails and camping. A map and recreational guide are recommended, and will be quite helpful. They can be obtained at the entrance, or in advance through the contact information in the Appendix. It is also possible to camp by permit on islands in Florida Bay, once reached by canoe or kayak, certainly an authentic Florida adventure. There are 99 miles of canoe trail in the Everglades known as the Wilderness Waterway.

Bicycling. While many of the roads and trails can be ridden, Long Pine Key, Shark Valley, and Snake Bight Trail offer the best opportunities.

Equestrian. A network of primitive roads on Long Pine Key are excellent for horse riding.

Hiking. In addition to the three bicycle trails and roadways, there are many other places to hike, short and long. Some of these include: Anhinga Trail, Gumbo Limbo Trail, Mahogany Hammock, Mrazek Pond, Nine Mile Pond, Pa-hay-okee Overlook, Pinelands Trail, and West Lake.

From US-1 in Homestead/Florida City, exit west on SR-9336 and continue to the entrance.

Top: **the central marsh of Everglades National Park.** *Middle:* **a carnivorous sundew plant from the Everglades flatwoods.**

THE HISTORIC EVERGLADES

At one time the Everglades was a vast and continuous system. Lake Okeechobee overflowed its banks and fed thousands of square miles as the sheet of water crept toward the sea. In some sense, most of South Florida, except the coasts and the Keys, could be considered part of the former Everglades.

The present-day Everglades is broken into various units. The best known is Everglades National Park. Other portions presented in this book include Everglades Water Conservation Area, Loxahatchee National Wildlife Refuge, and Lake Okeechobee. Many smaller portions of South Florida are in or on the edges of the Everglades. These include places such as Markham Park and Sawgrass Park.

Top: there is always something of interest in Everglades National Park, even for the most casual observer. Here, bicyclists admire a basking alligator (while maintaining a safe distance) at Shark Valley.

Center, left: hikers on the shady Snake Bight Trail near Flamingo.

Center, right: four German visitors enjoy the Florida sun while hiking along a Shark Valley loop trail.

Bottom, left: climbing the ramp to the observation tower at Shark Valley.

Top: many recreationists combine their love of nature with the exercise possibilities offered by hikes through the Everglades. Here, a group of hikers stops to document the variety of wild birds that can be observed, often at very close range. Because of the protection afforded wildlife in the Everglades, many creatures have become less wary of humans.

Above: a couple indulge their serious passion for bird photography.

Right: in the warm sunlight of late afternoon, a couple of hikers pause to admire the ibis perched on a nearby branch.

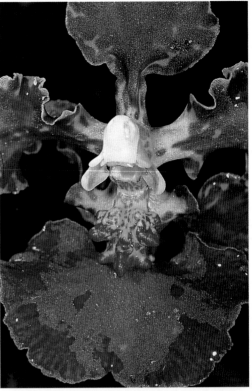

EVERGLADES WATER CONSERVATION AREA

(Broward, Dade, and Palm Beach counties, 884,680 acres, multi-use)

Approximately one-third of the historic Everglades has been set aside for water conservation. It is administered in three units: Water Conservation Areas 1, 2, and 3.

WCA-1 includes Loxahatchee National Wildlife Refuge and 30,000 acres in the Hillsboro Recreation Area. The two total 147,000 acres. The recreation area is the southern entrance to the refuge. This land is leased by the state to the federal government, and is located in Broward and Palm Beach counties. (For directions to Loxahatchee, see separate account.)

WCA-2 is 134,440 acres and located in Broward and Palm Beach counties also. WCA-3 is 603,240 acres and located in Broward and Dade counties. They are managed by the South Florida Water Management District and the Florida Fish and Wildlife Conservation Commission.

In general, trails in the water conservation areas are on levee dikes and access roads for official equipment. They have no shade, can be long and remote, and are similar. There are no water, no facilities, no fast food restaurants. The bikers, hikers, and riders who enjoy these trails are a different breed from the majority of trail users. These "trails" are not for casual, out-of-shape recreationists, at least not for long distances.

The question of equestrian use close to a public water supply arises from time to time. Horses are not allowed in area 1. They are allowed in areas 2 and 3. In reality, these are not the types of trails most horse riders are looking for, and horseback riding here is very infrequent. The most common usage at present, other than fishing, is bicycling.

The scenery is much like the Everglades National Park vistas, except for the impoundments. In the sawgrass, there are many birds, alligators, and water snakes.

While all the levees and roads can be ridden, here are four in particular that bicyclists have recommended.

WCA-2B has a 10.5 mile trail connecting Markham and Sawgrass Parks. These connections may be broken at times. Both Markham and Sawgrass have their own accounts and directions.

WCA-3B. A 13-mile loop, it can be reached from US-27 north of CR-820 by turning west on Griffin Road.

WCA-3B, L-28. A 17-mile ride each way, begins on US-41, west of Krome Avenue, at Fortymile Bend.

Water Conservation Areas 2A, and 3A North, 3A South, and 3B: contact Florida Fish and Wildlife Conservation Commission. Area 1 is controlled by the US Fish and Wildlife Service through the Loxahatchee National Wildlife Refuge. For the emaining areas, contact the water management district.

Top, left: **a painted bunting in the Everglades.**
Top, right: **a mule ear orchid.**

SAFETY AROUND ALLIGATORS

While Florida has no dangerous bears or wildcats, it does have alligators, several million of them. Large alligators do on occasion kill or maim careless people, but we are not normally on their diet. Usually we have intruded into the gator's life and habitat when there is an attack. The most dangerous alligators are likely to be those near some picnic area where they have previously been fed by uninformed humans. However, very large alligators never fed by human hands have attacked people, particularly swimmers.

These are the simple ways to protect yourself from alligators. Never disturb a nesting gator, and do not come between an alligator and the water. Avoid swimming in waters with alligators, and never, never grab a gator by the tail. As with all wild animals, given room and respect, there will be no safety question.

Like many predators, alligators may take the smallest, weakest member of a group. This includes small children and dogs. Taking a dog into an area with gators is a very bad idea. Swimming children should be watched in any waters, alligators or not, and children should be kept out of waters with gators. To protect everyone, including the gator that may otherwise be destroyed, never feed a gator (or any wildlife for that matter).

Above, left: the most practical way to experience the Fakahatchee Strand is to walk right into it.

Above, right: the scenic boardwalk under ancient cypress in Fakahatchee Strand State Preserve.

Below: typical vegetation along Janes Scenic Drive through Fakahatchee Strand State Preserve.

FAKAHATCHEE STRAND STATE PRESERVE

(Collier County, 74,000 acres, bicycling and hiking)

Reading that the Fakahatchee provided potential bicycle trips came first as quite a surprise to someone very familiar with it. After all, Janes Scenic Drive is an often dusty old lumbering road, and the spurs into the Fakahatchee botanical wonderland are more wet and muddy than dry. However, many enthusiasts believe the "Fak" provides terrific rides, and some have published accounts of the following: Jones Grade, a 6-mile grass ride; the 1-mile Mini-Tram Trail; the South Main Trail, 3 miles on crushed stone and grass; and, the West Main Trail, 3 miles on grass. Preserve officials, however, say the only designated area for bicycling is along Janes Scenic Drive, although they feel spurs 7 and 12 are also suitable. Visitors should judge for themselves.

For hiking, forget designated trails altogether. To see most of the wonders up close, it is necessary to walk off into the swamp. This should only be attempted by the experienced and well prepared, and then with a compass, or better yet, in the company of rangers, who conduct monthly walks.

A strand is a special kind of swamp, with a limestone bottom, an elongated shape, and deep sloughs, which combine to prevent frost and suppress fire. These conditions allow a wonderland of epiphytes, plants that grow on trees without harming them, including bromeliads and orchids. Up to 44 species of orchids have been recorded in the swamp, and the current count of bromeliad species is 14. There are both alligators and venomous snakes in the swamp, thus hikers must be aware.

It is amazing that the Fakahatchee still stands. In the 1940s, it was lumbered, leaving a vast muddy sea of stumps. The primary trees cut down were ancient cypress, more than 500 years old. A few of these giant trees can still be seen from a short boardwalk about 5 miles west of SR-29 on the north side of US-41.

Towering over the strand is a naturally occurring population of royal palms, overlooking a wild, tangled swamp dominated by trees, such as pond apple and swamp laurel oak.

Just south of Naples, I-75 bends eastward toward the Atlantic coast. From I-75, south (and east) of Naples, turn south on SR-29. Go 13 miles to the community of Copeland and turn west on Janes Scenic Drive and continue to the headquarters.

PC

HILLSBORO RECREATION AREA
See Everglades Water Conservation Area 1

HUGH BIRCH STATE RECREATION AREA
(Broward County, 180 acres, bicycling and hiking)

A short beach, a nature trail longer than a mile, and the paved road probably add up to over 3 miles. There are camping options at this very busy recreation area. In Ft. Lauderdale on A1A, turn west on East Sunrise Boulevard, and the entrance soon appears on the north side of the road.

JOHN PRINCE PARK
(Palm Beach County, 726 acres, bicycling and hiking)

One highlight of John Prince is Lake Osborne which attracts many waterbirds. Around it is a 5-mile trail used for bicycling, hiking, and jogging. There is a 1.4-mile fitness trail, and the Custard Apple Nature Trail. This is a popular campground with full services. From I-95 in Lake Worth, go west on 6th Avenue South. *Managed by: Palm Beach County.*

LAKE OKEECHOBEE
(Glades, Hendry, Martin, Okeechobee, and Palm Beach counties, bicycling and hiking)

The approximately 110 miles of the Florida Trail around Lake Okeechobee are mostly on the dikes. It is almost entirely a treeless bike ride or hike, so those attempting distance are advised to do so in the cooler months, or come prepared. It is possible to access it in small sections, one or two segments at a time.

Although a hypothetical trailhead is listed at Okee-Tantie Recreation Area southwest of the town of Okeechobee, what is the trailhead of a circle with over twenty different entry points? Access points are prominently announced on signs along the many roads around portions of Lake Okeechobee (including US-441, US-98, SR-15, SR-78, and US-27). Their locations can be obtained from the South Florida Water Management District at the address in the Appendix.

Lake Okeechobee appears vast enough to be confused with the ocean. It is not possible to see the opposite shore. Although relatively shallow, it is the second largest freshwater lake entirely in the US. Unfortunately, it is not in the best of health. Agricultural runoff and other pollutants threatens birds, including endangered species, and fish living in and around the lake.

Managed by: South Florida Water Management District.

(JOHN U.) LLOYD BEACH STATE RECREATION AREA
(Broward County, 253 acres, hiking)

In addition to 2.5 miles of first class beach, there is a 1-mile hiking trail. The recreation area is between the Intracoastal Waterway and the Atlantic Ocean. It is located on A1A north of Hollywood.

LARRY & PENNY THOMPSON PARK
(Dade County, 275 acres, bicycling and hiking)

This popular RV campground has a 5-mile trail, one way, used for biking, jogging, and walking, and 2.5 miles of bridle paths. In Miami, at 12451 Southwest 184th Street.

Above: **a jogger with his dog on top of the dike around Lake Okeechobee. More than 100 miles of dike are open for bicycling and jogging. The Florida Trail circles on the dike.**

LOVER'S KEY STATE RECREATION AREA
(Lee County, 712 acres, bicycling and hiking)

Visiting this recreation area will make many Floridians remember why they moved to Florida in the first place, and why they never left.

Approximately 2.5 miles of great beach is strewn with picturesque driftwood. The beach is bordered by passes north and south through which the tide surges between Estero Bay and the Gulf.

The entrance immediately south of the bridge over Big Carlos Pass has a 0.9-mile bike/hike in and out to beach access. There is a side bicycle route from that, and a paved path for bikes and foot traffic at the main entrance. To the south in the recreation area, two cement foot bridges lead over an estuary to the beach, while in the north there are two wooden bridges.

At the main entrance, 1.5 miles south of Big Carlos Pass, those who do not want to walk or bike can take a tram to the beach. There is also a bike path alongside the highway from Big Carlos to the bridge at New Pass. Kayaks and canoe rentals for exploring mangrove estuary are available at the concession.

Along the beaches are cord grass, palms, sea grapes, sea oats, and many other plants associated with beaches. Behind the beaches are mangroves. Porpoises are frequently seen, and raccoons are easily observed among the mangroves. During summer, this area sometimes is visited by spectacular concentrations of rays.

Location: south of Ft. Myers Beach across Carlos Pass, or north of Bonita Beach across New Pass. Ft. Myers Beach can be reached by taking the Daniels Parkway exit west from I-75. Turn southwest on Seven Mile Cypress and cross US-41. A prominent sign announces a turn toward both Ft. Myers Beach and Sanibel/Captiva. Another prominent sign indicates the turn south away from Sanibel/Captiva to Ft. Myers Beach.

Top: driftwood partially buried in the sand on the beach at Lovers Key State Recreation Area. The area has more than 2 miles of beach in a natural condition.

Left: a bridge leading from mangroves to the beach at Lovers Key State Recreation Area. There are three bridges and tram rides to the beach.

THE SIZE OF OKEECHOBEE

It is frequently stated that Lake Okeechobee is the second largest lake in the US. This is not correct. All the Great Lakes and the Great Salt Lake are larger. However, the Great Salt Lake is not freshwater, and only one of the Great Lakes is entirely in the US with no Canadian portion. Thus, it is proper to say that Okeechobee is the second largest freshwater lake entirely within the US borders. Okeechobee is a shallow lake, and does not hold as much water as many deep, glacial lakes. But Okeechobee is the mother of the Everglades. Its historic overflow created the Everglades.

(ARTHUR R. MARSHALL) LOXAHATCHEE NATIONAL WILDLIFE REFUGE

(Broward and Palm Beach counties, 147,368 acres, bicycling and hiking)

Loxahatchee is the most northern portion of the historic Everglades. It is a sanctuary for migratory birds. It has 6.4 miles of trails around a dike system. The refuge brings thousands of visitors annually to see the birds, alligators, and turtles.

A 12-mile section on levees from the head-quarters area to the Hillsboro Area was opened for mountain biking in October, 1999. No equestrian use is allowed.

Loxahatchee is Everglades Water Conservation Area 1 (WCA-1). There are three such areas, but WCA-1 is leased by the state to the federal government and operated as a national wildlife refuge by the US Fish and Wildlife Service.

The refuge is named in honor of Art Marshall, a passionate advocate for Florida wilderness and wildlife.

Located to the west of Boynton Beach. From I-95, go west on CR-804, then south on US-441 to the entrance on the west side of the road.

Top: sawgrass with tree islands in the distance at Loxahatchee Preserve Nature Center.

Left: red lichen is on trees along the boardwalk at Loxahatchee National Wildlife Refuge.

Below: a trail along the Loxahatchee River.

MARKHAM PARK
(Broward County, 665 acres, bicycling and hiking)

Just west of the junction of I-595, I-75, and SR-869, Markham sits almost under tall, concrete overpasses. It is also within a few miles of Sawgrass Mills Mall which draws shoppers who make cross-Florida trips to spend their money.

Within this county park and campground are 2-paved miles, and 4.3-miles of off-road trails used by bicyclists and walkers. This is a very popular and heavily-used park. The trails lead to levees and connect to Sawgrass Park, however the dike path is often broken by collapsed earth or bridge work. Both mahogany and gumbo limbo grow in the park.

Markham is located in Sunrise, 10 miles west of Ft. Lauderdale, near the Sawgrass Expressway, SR-869. From I-95, exit west at SW 136th Ave., go west on SR-84 for 2 miles. Markham is at Weston Road. *Managed by: Broward County.*

(JOHN D.) MACARTHUR BEACH STATE PARK
(Palm Beach County, 174 acres, hiking)

Three nature trails and a walk on the boardwak across Lake Worth Cove total 2 miles. Then there is almost 2 miles of fantastic Atlantic beach to stroll. From I-95, take PGA Boulevard east to A1A, then take A1A south.

OKEEHEELEE PARK
(Palm Beach County, 900 acres, bicycling and hiking)

This is a reclaimed shell quarry that offers 8.8 miles of biking and hiking, with a nature center. There is also a fitness trail. The Cholee trails also are directly across the street. This is also a large recreational complex, adjoining a public golf course. Not in any way a natural area, it is exceptionally popular for recreational use, especially bicycling. From I-95 in West Palm Beach, take Forest Hill Boulevard west 5 miles. Okeeheelee is to the north side, and Cholee is to the south. *Managed by: Palm Beach County.*

OLETA RIVER STATE RECREATION AREA
(Dade County, 1,052 acres, bicycling and hiking).

On Biscayne Bay, and mostly in the mangroves, are perhaps 5 miles of trails, mostly of crushed rock, used by bicyclists, joggers, and walkers. There is also beach to walk, mangrove estuary, and a 3.8-mile Oleta River Canoe Trail. From I-95, exit east on SR-826 (163rd Steet). The recreation area is at 3400 Northeast 163rd Street.

OVERSEAS HERITAGE TRAIL
(Monroe County, bicycling and hiking)

The proposed trail will extend 106.5 miles from Key Largo to Key West, some on the path of Flagler's old railway line. That line was destroyed in the infamous Labor Day Hurricane of 1935, along with hundreds of lives, including a rail car loaded with rescue workers which was swept to sea.

Smaller completed segments include: 1 mile asphalt on Fiesta Key; 2-miles asphalt and dirt on Cudjoe Key; 2.3-miles asphalt on Long and Conch keys; 4.4-miles asphalt on Lower Matecumbe Key; 2.3-miles of asphalt on Marathon; 0.5-mile asphalt on Missouri and Ohio keys; and 5-miles asphalt and dirt on Grassy Key and Walker's Island.

The Florida Keys are entirely in the tropical weather zone. Its seas are azure blue, and the Florida Current rips by the islands and under bridges. This is truly a grand bicycle ride or hike.

Managed by: Monroe County.

QUIET WATERS PARK
(Broward County, 425 acres, bicycling and hiking)

In the early morning and evening, hundreds of bicyclists (and some joggers) take to the winding bicycle paths in this park. There are beginning, intermediate, and advanced bicycle trails. Included in the potential 6 miles are some pretty bumpy climbs over and down the roots of Australian pines. "Down" in many cases means short falls. There is one steep climb (called "the mountain," by users) requiring a good head start. Located in Pompano Beach. From I-95, take 10th Street West to North Powerline Road. The park is 0.5 mile up this road on the west side. If the turn at Powerline is missed, the motorist is liable to end up on a toll road or may be forced to make an illegal u-turn, risking safety and fines. *Managed by Broward County.*

Top: cyclist in Quiet Waters Park.
Above, left: gumbo limbo and mahogany trees in Markham park.
Above, right: a paved trail in Okeeheelee Park.

SANIBEL/CAPTIVA TRAIL
(Lee County, 1,100 acres, hiking)

Ten short trails combine for a little over 4 miles. These trails are for hiking, but Sanibel offers miles and miles of bicycle paths. The trails are part of the Sanibel-Captiva Conservation Foundation, which has a nature center at 333 Sanibel-Captiva Road, 1 mile west of Tarpon Bay Road.

Habitats: beach, hammock, and mangroves. From I-75 in Ft. Myers, exit on Daniels Parkway west, and follow directional signs to Sanibel.

SAWGRASS PARK
(Broward County, bicycling and hiking)

Sawgrass is easily missed. Campers and trailers make it look like a campground. Compared to many other areas, it is small. It is a commercial location with boat docks, airboat rides, a baithouse, restaurant, and even a tiny zoo, including a reticulated python. To top off this un-parklike picture, the zoo and docks are sometimes surrounded by vultures.

Sawgrass Park offers access to miles of levees into the Everglades Conservation Area. It would be possible to travel on the levees to Markham Park to the east, except the path is sometimes broken. Out on the lonely, shadeless dikes, it is possible to see alligators, birds, deer, wild pigs, and smaller wildlife. While the water conservation areas (not leased to the federal government) are multi-use, there is hardly sufficient room through the gate for anything other than a bicycle or a person.

From Ft. Lauderdale, take I-595 west toward the junction with I-75. Just before the North I-75 Tollroad, exit north on US-27. Sawgrass is on the east side of the road within 3 miles.
Managed by: Broward County.

SOUTH DADE GREENWAYS NETWORK
(Dade County, bicycling and hiking)

Imagine 194 miles of bicycle and pedestrian paths, the vast majority of them paved! This is the eventual plan, and substantial portions have been completed including: Biscayne, Everglades, Keys, Krome, Mowry, Princeton, South Dade, and Southern Glades trails, with additional sections under way for the Oleta River, Snake Creek, and a Beach Walk Corridor along Miami Beach. This vast system of trails will be best explored with advance information in the form of a brochure indicating trailheads.
Mananged by: South Dade Greenway Network.

SOUTHERN GLADES WILDLIFE AND ENVIRONMENTAL AREA
(Dade County, 30,080 acres, multi-use)

This area has two multi-use trails totaling 16 miles on levees and roads. As might be expected, this is a very wet area, containing marsh with sawgrass, and swamp. It contains typical Everglades sights, including alligators, birds, and sawgrass. From US-1, go west on Work Camp Road, south of Homestead on the way to the Keys.
Managed by: Florida Fish and Wildlife Conservation Commission.

Top: a couple walking along the beach on Sanibel Island. Sanibel and adjoining Captiva have many miles of beach.

Below: great blue herons are common along Florida's waterways.

PC

SHORTER SOUTH FLORIDA TRAILS

CORKSCREW SWAMP SANCTUARY
(Collier County)

The Corkscrew is a wonderful place for nature enthusiasts and birders. This Audubon preserve has 2.5 miles of boardwalk through the oldest remaining cypress stand and swamp in South Florida. From I-75, near Naples, go east on SR-846, 15 miles to Sanctuary Road.

DELNOR-WIGGINS PASS STATE RECREATION AREA
(Collier County)

With condominiums rising on the north, east, and south, many might shy away from Delnor-Wiggins, but that would be unfortunate. While summer beaches might be clogged with sunbathers, on winter mornings the beach belongs to gulls, pelicans, sandpipers, terns, and walkers. The roads belong to bicyclists, joggers, and roller-bladers. In addition to the beach, there are mangroves on the pass and bay sides. South of Bonita Springs, north of Naples. From US-41, go west on CR-901 to the recreation area.

FLORIDA PANTHER NATIONAL WILDLIFE REFUGE
(Collier County)

In the past, the refuge was entirely closed to the general public, but a short nature trail has been constructed along SR-29 north of I-75. The chances of seeing a panther are exceptionally slim, and the bugs here frequently have visitors slapping each other like Curly, Larry, and Moe. Still, it is panther country.

JOHN PENNEKAMP CORAL REEF STATE PARK
(Monroe County)

There are two short loop trails totaling about 1 mile. One is through tropical hammock, while the other passes through mangrove. But the reason to come to Pennnekamp is not merely the trails, but the marvelous coral reefs, revealed during dive and glass-bottom boat trips. Pennekamp plays a major role in educating the public about one of our most treasured ecosystems - coral reefs. Located in Key Largo, prominently marked, to the east of US-1.

LAKES PARK
(Lee County)

Paved paths 2.5 miles long have been built around reclaimed rock mining pits that are now lakes. Many bicyclists, joggers, and walkers enjoy the view of anhingas, coots, cormorants, ibis, herons, and many other birds. While some naturalists might shake their heads at the three curses of South Florida (Australian pine, Brazilian pepper, and melaleuca), the value of this small park to Lee County residents and tourists is great. From I-75, go west on Daniels Parkway, then southwest on Seven Mile Cypress, and across US-41. Within a mile, the entrance is on the north side of the road.

LIGNUMVITAE KEY STATE BOTANICAL SITE
(Monroe County)

This small, wild island is mostly a dense richness of trees, including lignumvitae, an understory tree that has exceptionally hard

Above: **key deer are about the size of a German shepherd and seem to have little fear of humans.**

wood. The ranger-guided walk is 1 mile when the mosquitoes are intolerable, and a rare 2 miles otherwise. Located in Florida Bay, from MM 78.5. Boat transportation is available from Upper and Lower Matecumbe keys.

NATIONAL KEY DEER REFUGE
(Monroe County)

Although Jack Watson Nature Trail is only 0.66 of a mile, it is worth the trip just to see a Key deer. The white-tailed deer in the lower keys evolved into this small sub-species, better able to tolerate sparse food and water, and greater heat. From US-1 on Big Pine Key, go north 3.5 miles on Key Deer Boulevard.

SIX MILE CYPRESS SLOUGH PRESERVE
(Lee County)

A boardwalk winds past lakes where alligators and birds are plentiful. The boardwalk also passes through cypress swamp dense with ferns and profuse with bromeliads - a tropical wonderland. The boardwalk has expanded over a few years from very short to approaching 2 miles and may expand futher. Exit 1-75 west at Daniels Parkway and turn north at Seven Mile Cypress. Travel about 2 miles. The entrance is on the east side of the road, prominently marked.

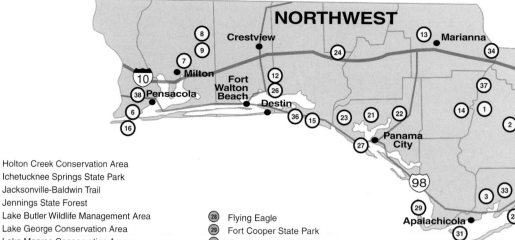

NORTHWEST

1. Apalachicola Bluffs and Ravines
2. Apalachicola National Forest
3. Apalachicola River Wildlife and Environmental Area
4. Aucilla Wildlife Management Area
5. Big Bend Wildlife Management Area
6. Big Lagoon State Recreation Area
7. Blackwater Heritage State Trail
8. Blackwater River State Forest
9. Blackwater River State Park
10. Econfina River State Park
12. Eglin Air Force Base
13. Florida Caverns State Park
14. Florida River Island Trail
15. Grayton Beach State Recreation Area
16. Gulf Islands National Seashore
17. Lake Talquin State Forest
18. Maclay Gardens State Park
19. Ochlockonee River State Park
20. Phipps Park
21. Pine Log State Forest
22. Pitt Springs
23. Point Washington State Forest
24. Ponce De Leon Springs State Recreation Area
25. River Bluff State Picnic Site
26. Rocky Bayou State Recreation Area
27. St. Andrews State Recreation Area
28. St. George Island State Park
29. St. Joseph Peninsula State Park
30. St. Marks National Wildlife Refuge
31. St. Vincent National Wildlife Refuge
32. Tallahassee-St. Marks State Trail
33. Tate's Hell State Forest
34. Three Rivers State Recreation Area
35. Tom Brown Park
36. Topsail Hill State Preserve
37. Torreya State Park
38. University of West Florida
39. Wakulla Springs State Park

NORTH

1. Alapaha River Basin Conservation Area
2. Allardt Tract
3. Allen Mill Pond
4. Amelia Island State Recreation Area
5. Anastasia State Park
6. Andrews Wildlife Management Area
7. Bayard Conservation Area
8. Bay Creek Conservation Area
9. Beardsley Tract
10. Benton Conservation Area
11. Big Shoals Public Lands
12. Big Talbot Island State Park
13. Black Creek Ravines Conservation Area
14. Branford Rail-to-Trail
15. Brantley Tract
16. Bulow Creek State Park
17. Bulow Plantation Ruins State Historial Site
18. Camp Blanding
19. Camp Branch Conservation Area
20. Caravelle Wildlife Management Area
21. Cary State Forest
22. Cedar Key Scrub State Reserve
23. Cypress Creek Conservation Area
24. Deleon Springs State Recreation Area
25. Depot Trail
26. Devils Millhopper State Geological Site
27. Dunns Creek Conservation Area
28. Emeralda Marsh Conservation Area
29. Etoniah Creek State Forest
30. Fanning Springs State Recreation Area
31. Faver-Dykes State Park
32. Flat Island Preserve
33. Fort Clinch State Park
34. Fox Tract
35. Gainesville-Hawthorne State Trail
36. Gar Pond
37. Goethe State Forest
38. Gold Head Branch State Park
39. Guana River State Park/ Guana River Wildlife Management Area
40. Gum Root Swamp Conservation Area
41. Hanna Park
42. Heart Island Conservation Area
43. Holton Creek Conservation Area
44. Ichetucknee Springs State Park
45. Jacksonville-Baldwin Trail
46. Jennings State Forest
47. Lake Butler Wildlife Management Area
48. Lake George Conservation Area
49. Lake Monroe Conservation Area
50. Lake Woodruff National Wildlife Refuge
51. Little Talbot Island State Park
52. Little Shoals Tract
53. Lochloosa Conservation Area
54. Lower Suwannee National Wildlife Refuge
55. Manatee Springs State Park
56. Mattair Springs Tract/Woods Ferry Tract
57. Moses Creek Conservation Area
58. Ocala National Forest
59. Ocklawaha Prairie Restoration Area
60. O'Leno State Park
61. Osceola National Forest
62. Paynes Prairie State Preserve
63. Pellicer Creek Conservation Area
64. Rainbow Springs State Park
65. Ralph E. Simmons Memorial State Forest
66. Ravine State Garden
67. Rice Creek Sanctuary
68. River Rise State Preserve
69. Ruth Springs Tract
70. San Felasco Hammock State Preserve
71. Sawgrass Island Preserve
72. Silver River State Park
73. Steinhatchee Falls Wildlife Management Area
74. Stephen Foster State Folk Culture Center
75. Stokes Landing Conservation Area
76. Sunnyhill Restoration Area
77. Suwannee River State Park.
78. Suwannee Springs, Linville Tract
79. Talbot GeoPark
80. Tiger Bay State Forest
81. Tomoka State Park
82. Twin Rivers State Forest
83. Waldo Rail-to-Trail
84. Washington Oaks State Gardens
85. Welaka State Forest
86. White Springs Tract

CENTRAL

1. Alderman-Ford Park
2. Avon Park Bombing Range
3. Balm-Boyette Scrub Preserve
4. Blue Cypress Conservation Area
5. Blue Spring State Park
6. Boyd Hill Nature Park
7. Buck Lake Conservation Area
8. Bull Creek Wildlife Management Area
9. Cady Way Trail
10. Caladesi Island State Park
11. Canaveral Marshes Conservation Area
12. Canaveral National Seashore
13. Carlton Reserve
14. Carlton Tract
15. Carter Road Park
16. Catfish Creek State Preserve
17. Chassahowitzka Wildlife Management Area
18. Chuluota Wilderness Area
19. Cross Seminole Trail
20. Cypress Creek Wellfield
21. Dead River Site
22. Disney Wilderness Preserve
23. Duette Park
24. Econ River Wilderness Area
26. Flagler Trail
27. Flatwoods Park
28. Flying Eagle
29. Fort Cooper State Park
30. Fort DeSoto Park
31. Fort Drum Marsh Conservation Area
32. Fort Pierce Inlet State Recreation Area (Including Jack Island)
33. Friendship Trail
34. Gasparilla Island State Recreation Area
35. Green Swamp
36. Half Moon Wildlife Management Area
37. Halpata Tastanaki Preserve
38. Hal Scott Regional Preserve and Park
39. Hickory Hammock
40. Highlands Hammock State Park
41. Hillsborough River State Park
42. Hobe Sound National Wildlife Refuge
43. Honeymoon Island State Recreation Area
44. Hontoon Island State Park
45. Jack Creek
46. Jay Blanchard Park/Little Econ Greenway
47. Jonathan Dickinson State Park
48. Kicco Wildlife Management Area
49. Kissimmee Prairie State Preserve
50. Lake Apopka Restoration Area
51. Lake Jessup Wilderness Area
52. Lake Louisa State Park
53. Lake Kissimmee State Park
54. Little Manatee River State Park
55. Lake Manatee State Recreation Area
56. Lake Marion Creek Management Area
57. Lake Minneola Scenic Trail
58. Lake Panasoffkee Project
59. Lake Proctor Wilderness Area
60. Lake Wales Ridge State Forest
61. Lettuce Lake Park
62. Little-Big Econ State Forest
63. Lower Hillsborough Flood Detention Area
64. Lower Wekiva River State Reserve
65. Medard Park
66. Merritt Island National Wildlife Refuge
67. Morris Bridge Bicycle Area
68. Myakka Prairie
69. Myakka River State Park
70. Myakka State Forest
71. Oscar Scherer State Park
72. Orlando Wetlands Park/Orlando Wilderness Park
73. Pinellas Trail
74. Potts Preserve
75. River Lake Conservation Area
76. Rock Springs Run State Reserve
77. Ross Prairie State Forest
78. Rye Wilderness Park
79. Savannas State Preserve
80. Sargeant Park
81. Sebastian Inlet State Recreation Area
82. Seminole Ranch Conservation Area
83. Seminole State Forest
84. Seminole-Wekiva Trail
85. Split Oak Forest Mitigation Park
86. Spruce Creek Preserve
87. St. Lucie Inlet State Preserve
88. St. Sebastian River State Buffer Preserve
89. Starkey Wilderness Park
90. Suncoast Parkway
91. Sunnyhill Restoration Area
92. Tampa Bypass Canal
93. Tenoroc Fish Management Area
94. Three Forks Marsh Conservation Area

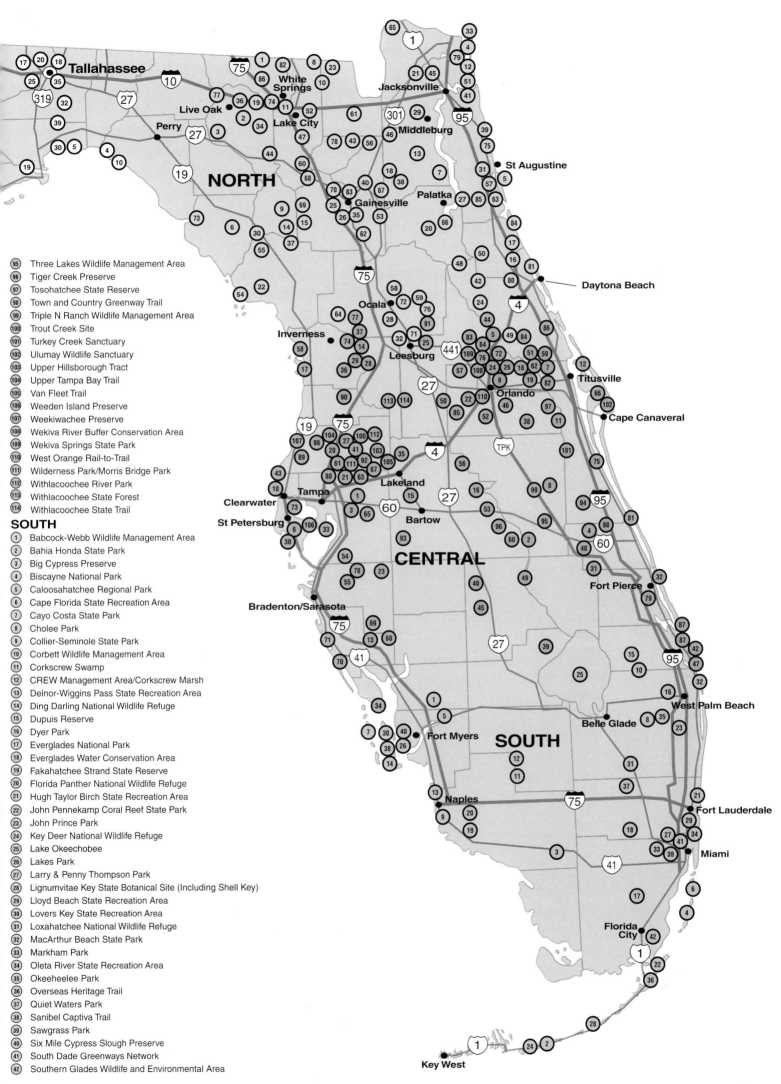

95 Three Lakes Wildlife Management Area
96 Tiger Creek Preserve
97 Tosohatchee State Reserve
98 Town and Country Greenway Trail
99 Triple N Ranch Wildlife Management Area
100 Trout Creek Site
101 Turkey Creek Sanctuary
102 Ulumay Wildlife Sanctuary
103 Upper Hillsborough Tract
104 Upper Tampa Bay Trail
105 Van Fleet Trail
106 Weeden Island Preserve
107 Weekiwachee Preserve
108 Wekiva River Buffer Conservation Area
109 Wekiva Springs State Park
110 West Orange Rail-to-Trail
111 Wilderness Park/Morris Bridge Park
112 Withlacoochee River Park
113 Withlacoochee State Forest
114 Withlacoochee State Trail

SOUTH

1 Babcock-Webb Wildlife Management Area
2 Bahia Honda State Park
3 Big Cypress Preserve
4 Biscayne National Park
5 Caloosahatchee Regional Park
6 Cape Florida State Recreation Area
7 Cayo Costa State Park
8 Cholee Park
9 Collier-Seminole State Park
10 Corbett Wildlife Management Area
11 Corkscrew Swamp
12 CREW Management Area/Corkscrew Marsh
13 Delnor-Wiggins Pass State Recreation Area
14 Ding Darling National Wildlife Refuge
15 Dupuis Reserve
16 Dyer Park
17 Everglades National Park
18 Everglades Water Conservation Area
19 Fakahatchee Strand State Reserve
20 Florida Panther National Wildlife Refuge
21 Hugh Taylor Birch State Recreation Area
22 John Pennekamp Coral Reef State Park
23 John Prince Park
24 Key Deer National Wildlife Refuge
25 Lake Okeechobee
26 Lakes Park
27 Larry & Penny Thompson Park
28 Lignumvitae Key State Botanical Site (Including Shell Key)
29 Lloyd Beach State Recreation Area
30 Lovers Key State Recreation Area
31 Loxahatchee National Wildlife Refuge
32 MacArthur Beach State Park
33 Markham Park
34 Oleta River State Recreation Area
35 Okeeheelee Park
36 Overseas Heritage Trail
37 Quiet Waters Park
38 Sanibel Captiva Trail
39 Sawgrass Park
40 Six Mile Cypress Slough Preserve
41 South Dade Greenways Network
42 Southern Glades Wildlife and Environmental Area

MAILING ADDRESSES,
PHONE NUMBERS,
CONTACT INFORMATION.
Please note that due to rapid growth, both area codes and zip codes may change.

Anastasia State Park
1340A A1A South
St. Augustine FL 32084
904-461-2033
904-461-2006 (fax)

Apalachicola Bluffs and Ravines
The Nature Conservancy
PO Box 393
Bristol FL 32321
850-643-2756
850-643-5246 (fax)

Apalachicola National Forest
Apalachicola Ranger District
PO Box 579
Bristol FL 32321
850-643-2282
850-643-2284 (fax)

Wakulla Ranger District
1773 Crawfordville Highway
Crawfordville FL 32327
850-926-3561
850-926-1904 (fax)

Avon Park Bombing Range
Natural Resource Manager
56 CSS-DEN
236 South Boulevard
Avon Park AFB FL 33825
863-452-4254
863-452-4119 Ext 5 (recording)
863-452-4161 (fax)

Bahia Honda State Park
36850 Overseas Highway
Big Pine Key FL 33043
305-872-3897
305-292-6857 (fax)

Big Cypress National Preserve
HCR-61
Ochopee FL 34141
941-695-2000
941-695-3493 (fax)

**Big Lagoon State
Recreation Area**
12301 Gulf Beach Highway
Pensacola FL 32507
850-492-1595

Big Shoals Public Lands
7620 133d Road
Live Oak FL 32322
904-208-1460
904-208-1465 (fax)

Biscayne National Park
PO Box 1369
Homestead FL 33090
305-230-7275
305-230-1190 (fax)

Blackwater River State Forest
11650 Munson Highway
Milton FL 32570
850-957-6140
850-957-6143 (fax)

Blackwater River State Park
Blackwater Heritage State Trail
7720 Deaton Ridge Road
Holt FL 32564
850-983-5363

Blue Spring State Park
2100 French Avenue
Orange City FL 32763
904-775-3663
904-775-7794 (fax)

Boyd Hill Nature Park
1101 Country Club Way South
St Petersburg FL 33705
727-893-7326
727-893-7720 (fax)

**Brevard County
Parks and Recreation**
950 Kiwanis Island Park Road
Merritt Island FL 32953
407-868-1123
407-455-1384 (fax)
www.brevardparks.com

Caladesi Island State Park
Gulf Islands GeoPark
#1 Causeway Boulevard
Dunedin FL 34698
727-469-5942
727-469-5703 (fax)

Camp Blanding
Range Control
Rt 1 Box 465
Starke FL 32091
904-533-3351
904-533-3489 (fax)

Canaveral National Seashore
308 Julia Street
Titusville FL 32796
407-267-1110
407-264-2906 (fax)

**Cape Florida State
Recreation Area**
1200 South Crandon Boulevard
Key Biscayne FL 33149
305-361-5811

Cary State Forest
8719 West Beaver Street
Jacksonville FL 32220
904-266-5021
904-266-5021 (fax)

Catfish Creek State Preserve
Contact Lake Kissimmee
State Park

Cayo Costa State Park
PO Box 1150
Boca Grande FL 33921
941-964-0375
Boat Concession: 941-283-0015

**Cedar Key Scrub State Preserve
Waccassa Bay State Preserve**
PO Box 187
Cedar Key FL 32625
352-543-5567

**Carter Road Park
Polk County
Parks and Recreation**
515 East Boulevard Street
Bartow FL 33830
863-534-4340

**City of Gainesville
Parks and Recreation**
PO Box 490
Gainesville FL 32602
352-324-5074

**City of Jacksonville
Parks and Recreation**
851 North Market Street
Jacksonville FL 32202
904-630-4100
904-360-3567 (fax)

**City of Tallahassee
Parks and Recreation**
912 Myers Park Drive
Tallahassee FL 32301
850-891-3975
850-891-0959 (fax)

Collier Seminole State Park
20200 Tamiami Trail East
Naples FL 34114
941-394-3397
941-394-5113 (fax)

Cross Florida Greenway
Ocala Field Office
Office of Greenways
8282 Southeast Highway 314
Ocala FL 34470
352-236-7143
352-236-9121 (fax)

Dade County
Bicycle/Pedestrian Coordinator
111 NW First Street Suite 910
Miami FL 33128

**DeLeon Springs
State Recreation Area**
PO Box 1338
DeLeon Springs FL 32130
904-985-4212

**Department of Enviornmental
Protection**
Division of Parks and Recreation
3900 Commonwealth Boulevard
Tallahassee FL 32399
850-488-9872
850-922-4925 (fax)
http://www.dep.state.fl.us/parks

**Ding Darling
National Wildlife Refuge**
1 Wildlife Drive
Sanibel FL 33957
941-472-1100
941-472-4061 (fax)

**Disney Wilderness Preserve
Nature Conservancy**
2700 Scrub Jay Trail
Kissimmee FL 34739
407-935-0002
407-935-0005 (fax)

**Division of Forestry
Florida Department of
Agriculture**
3125 Conner Boulevard
Tallahassee FL 32399
850-488-8180
850-921-8305
www.fl-dof.com

Duette Park
2649 Rawls Road RR2
Bowling Green FL 33834
941-776-2295

Econfina River State Park
Tallahassee/St Marks GEOPark
1022 DeSoto Park Drive
Tallahassee FL 32301
850-922-6007
850-488-0366 (fax)

Eglin AFB Natural Resources
Jackson Guard
107 Hwy 85 North
Niceville FL 32578
850-882-4164

Etoniah Creek State Forest
PO Box 174
Welaka FL 32193
904-329-3772
904-329-3772 (fax)

Everglades National Park
40001 SR-9336
Homestead FL 33034
305-242-7700
305-242-7711 (fax)
www.nps.govever

**Fakahatchee Strand
State Preserve**
PO Box 548
Copeland FL 34137
941-695-4593
941-695-4947 (fax)

**Fanning Springs
State Recreation Area**
c/o Manatee Springs State Park
Suwannee Basin GeoPark
11650 NW 115th Street
Chiefland FL 32626
352-463-3420
352-493-6089 (fax)

Florida Caverns State Park
3345 Cavern Road
Marianna FL 32446
850-482-1228
850-482-9114 (fax)

Florida Bicycle Association
PO Box 1547
Orlando, FL 32802
www.floridabicycle.org

**Florida Fish and Wildlife
Conservation Commission**
620 South Meridian Street
Farris Bryant Building
Tallahassee, FL 323990-1600
www.state.fl.us/fwc

Florida Trail Association
5415 SW 13th Street
Gainesville FL 32608
352-378-8823
Toll Free (800) 343-1882
www.florida-trail.org

**Ft. Pierce Inlet
State Recreation Area**
905 Shorewinds Drive
Ft Pierce FL 34949
561-461-3059

Ft. Clinch State Park
2601 Atlantic Avenue
Fernandina Beach FL 32034
904-277-7274
904-277-7225 (fax)

Ft. Cooper State Park
3100 S Old Floral City Road
Inverness FL 32550
352-726-0315
352-726-6959 (fax)

**Gasparilla Island
State Recreation Area**
PO Box 1150
Boca Grande FL 33921
941-964-0375
941-964-1154 (fax)

Goethe State Forest
8250 SE CR-336
Dunnellon FL 34431
352-447-2202
352-447-1358 (fax)

Gold Head Branch
State Park
6239 SR-21
Keystone Heights FL 32656
352-473-4701
352-473-0827 (fax)

Grayton Beach
State Recreation Area
357 Main Park Road
Santa Rosa Beach FL 32459
850-231-4210

Guana River State Park
2690 S Ponte Vedra Boulevard
Ponte Vedra Beach FL 32082
904-825-5071

Gulf Islands National Seashore
1801 Gulf Breeze Parkway
Gulf Breeze FL 32561
850-934-2600
850-932-8654 (fax)

(Kathryn Abbey) Hanna Park
504 Wonderland Avenue
Jacksonville, FL 32227
904-249-4700
904-247-8688 (fax)

Highlands Hammock State Park
5931 Hammock Road
Sebring FL 33872
863-386-6094
863-386-6095

**Hillsborough County
Parks and Recreation**
1102 East River Cove Drive
Tampa FL 33604
813-975-2160

Hillsborough River State Park
15402 US 301 North
Thonotosassa FL 33592
813-987-6771
813-987-6773 (fax)

**Hobe Sound
National Wildlife Refuge**
PO Box 645
Hobe Sound FL 33475
561-732-3684
561-545-7572 (fax)

Honeymoon Island State Park
Gulf Coast GeoPark
#1 Causeway Boulevard
Dunedin FL 34698

727-469-5942
727-469-5703 (fax)

Hontoon Island State Park
2309 River Ridge Road
Deland FL 32720
904-736-5309

Ichetucknee Springs State Park
Rt-2, Box 5355
Ft. White FL 32038
904-497-2511
904-497-3095 (fax)

Jacksonville-Baldwin Trail
Department of Parks
555 W 44th Street
Jacksonville FL 32208
904-630-5400

Jennings State Forest
1337 Long Horn Road
Middleburg FL 32068
904-291-5530
904-291-5537 (fax)

Jonathan Dickinson State Park
16540 Southeast Federal Highway
Hobe Sound FL 33455
561-546-2771

Kissimmee Prairie State Preserve
33104 NW 192 Avenue
Okeechobee FL 34972
863-462-5360
863-462-5276 (fax)

Lake County Water Authority
107 North Lake Avenue
Tavares FL 32778
352-343-3777
352-343-4259 (fax)

Lake Kissimmee State Park
14248 Camp Mack Road
Lake Wales FL 33853
863-696-1112
863-696-2656 (fax)

Lake Louisa State Park
12549 State Park Drive
Clermont FL 34711
352-394-3969

Lake Talquin State Forest
865 Geddie Road
Tallahassee FL 32304
850-488-1871
850-922-2107 (fax)

Lake Wales Ridge State Forest
452 School Bus Road
Frostproof FL 33843
863-635-7801
863-635-7837 (fax)

**Lake Woodruff
National Wildlife Refuge**
PO Box 488
DeLeon Springs FL 32038
904-985-4673

Larry & Penny Thompson Park
12451 SW 184 Street
Miami FL 33177
305-232-1049

Lee County Parks & Recreation
3410 Palm Beach
Ft Myers FL 32916
941-338-3300
www.lee-county.com/parks&rec

Little Big Econ Sate Forest
1350 Snowhill Road
Geneva FL 32732
407-971-3503
407-971-3504 (fax)

**Little Manatee
State Recreation Area**
215 Lightfoot Road
Wimauma FL 33598
941-671-5005

**Lloyd Beach State Recreation
Area**
6503 North Ocean Drive
Dania FL 33004
954-923-2833

Lovers Key State Recreation Area
8700 Estero Boulevard
Fort Myers Beach FL 33931
941-463-4588
941-463-8851 (fax)

**Lower Suwannee
National Wildlife Refuge**
16450 NW 31st Place
Chiefland FL 32626
352-493-0238
352-493-1935 (fax)

**Lower Wekiva State Preserve
Wekiwa Springs State Park**
1800 Wekiva Circle
Apopka FL 32712
407-884-2006

**Loxahatchee
National Wildlife Refuge**
10216 Lee Road
Boynton Beach FL 33437
561-734-8303
561-369-7190 (fax)

**MacArthur Beach
State Recreation Area**
10900 State Route 703
North Palm Beach FL 33408
561-624-9650

Maclay Gardens State Park
3540 Thomasville Road
Tallahassee FL 32308
850-487-4556

Manatee Springs State Park
11650 NW 115th Street
Chiefland FL 32626
352-493-6072
352-493-6089 (fax)

**Merritt Island
National Wildlife Refuge**
PO Box 6504
Titusville FL 32782
407-861-0662
407-861-1276 (fax)

Monroe County
2798 Overseas Highway Suite 410

Marathon FL 33050-4277
Myakka River State Park
13207 SR-82
Sarasota FL 34241
941-361-6511
941-361-6501 (fax)

Myakka State Forest
4273 53d Avenue East
Bradenton FL 34203
941-751-7629
941-751-7631 (fax)

**Northwest Florida Water
Management District**
Rt 1 Box 3100
Havanna FL 32333
850-539-5999
www.nwwmd.state.fl.us

Ocala National Forest
Lake George Ranger District
17147 E Hwy-40
Silver Springs FL 34488
352-625-2520
3562-625-7556 (fax)

Seminole Ranger District
40929 SR-19
Umatilla FL 32784
352-669-3153
352-669-2385 (fax)

Ochlockonee River State Park
PO Box 5
Sopchoppy FL 32358
850-962-2771

**Oleta River State
Recreation Area**
3400 NE 163d Street
North Miami Beach FL 37160
305-919-1846

**O'Leno State Park
River Rise State Preserve**
Rt 2 Box 307
High Springs FL 32643
904-454-1853
904-454-2565 (fax)

**Orange County
Parks and Recreation**
4801 West Colonial Drive
Orlando FL 32808
407-836-6200
407-836-6210 (fax)

**Orlando Wetlands Park
Orlando Wilderness
Environmental Services**
City of Orlando
5100 L. B. McLeod Road
Orlando FL 32811
407-246-2213

Oscar Scherer State Park
1843 South Tamiami Trail
Osprey FL 34229
941-483-5956
941-480-3007 9 (fax)

Osceola National Forest
PO Box 70
Olustee FL 32072
904-752-2577
904-752-7437 (fax)

**Palm Beach County
Parks and Recreation**
2700 6th Ave S
Lake Worth FL 33461
561-966-6600
561-642-2640 (fax)
www.co.palm-beach.fl.us

**Pasco County
Parks and Recreation**
4111 Land O'Lakes Boulevard
Land of Lakes FL 34639
813-929-1260
813-929-1258 (fax)

Paynes Prairie State Preserve
100 Savannah Boulevard
Micanopy FL 32667
352-466-3397
352-446-4297 (fax)

Pine Log State Forest
715 West 15th Street
Panama City FL 32401
850-747-5639
850-872-4879 (fax)

**Pinellas County
Parks and Recreation**
631 Chestnut Street
Clearwater FL 33756
727-464-3347
727-464-3379 (fax)

Point Washington State Forest
715 West 15th Street
Panama City FL 32401
850-747-5639
850-872-4879 (fax)

Quiet Waters Park
401 South Powerline Road
Deerfield Beach FL 33442
954-360-1315

Rainbow Springs State Park
19158 SW 81st Place Road
Dunnellon FL 34432
352-489-8503
352-465-7855 (fax)

**Ralph E. Simmons
Memorial State Forest**
Rt 5 Box 9821 Hillard FL 32046
904-845-3597
904-845-4508 (fax)

Rice Creek Sanctuary
Georgia Pacific Paper Company
PO Box 158
East Palatka FL 32121

**Rock Springs Run
State Reserve**
Wekiva Basin Geo Park
1800 Wekiwa Circle
Apopka FL 32712
407-884-2009.

**San Felasco Hammock
State Preserve**
4732 Millhopper Road
Gainesville FL 32606
904-462-7905
904-462-7297 (fax)

Savannas State Reserve
905 Shorewinds Drive
Ft Pierce FL 34949
407-340-7530

126

**Sebastian Inlet State
Recreation Area**
9700 South A1A
Melbourne Beach FL 32951
561-984-4852

Seminole County
Natural Lands Program
1101 E 1st Street
Sanford FL 32771
407-665-7352
407-665-7385 (fax)
www.co.seminole.fl.us

Seminole State Forest
9610 CR-44
Leesburg FL 34788
352-360-6675

South Dade Greenways
Miami-Dade County
111 Northwest First Street
Miami, FL 32138
305-740-9007

**South Florida Water
Management District**
PO Box 24680
West Palm Beach FL 33416
1-561-686-8800
www.sfwmd.gov

**Southwest Florida Water
Management District**
2379 Broad Street
Brooksville FL 34609
352-796-7211
www.swfwmd.state.fl.us

**Spirit of the Suwannee
Music Park**
3076 95th Drive
Live Oak FL 32060
904-364-1683
904-364-2998 (fax)

**St. Andrews State
Recreation Area**
4607 State Park Lane
Panama City FL 32408
850-233-5140

St. George Island State Park
1900 E Gulf Beach Avenue
St George Island FL 32338
850-927-2111

**St. Johns River Water
Management District**
PO Box 1429 Palatka FL 32178
904-329-4500
904-329-4848 (fax)
http://sjr.state.fl.us

St. Joseph Peninsula State Park
8899 Cape San Blas Rd
Port St. Joe FL 32456
850-227-1327
850-227-1448 (fax)

**St. Marks National
Wildlife Refuge**
Box 68 St. Marks FL 32355
850-925-6121
850-925-6930 (fax)
http://saint-marks.fws.gov

**St. Vincents National
Wildlife Refuge**
PO Box 447
Apalachicola FL 32329
850-663-8808
850-653-9893 (fax)

Stephen Foster Cultural Center
PO Drawer G
White Springs FL 32096
904-397-2733
904-397-4262 (fax)

Suwannee Bicycle Association
PO Box 247
White Springs FL 32096
904-397-2347
www.suwanneebike.org

Suwannee River State Park
Rt 8 Box 297
Live Oak FL 32060
904-362-2746
904-364-1614 (fax)

**Suwannee River Water
Management District**
9225 CR-49
Live Oak FL 32060
904-362-1001
www.srwmd.state.fl.us

Talbot GeoPark
12157 Heckscher Drive
Ft. George Island FL 32226
904-251-2323
904-251-2325 (fax)

**Tallahassee-St Marks
State Trail**
Tallahassee-St Marks GeoPark
1022 DeSoto Park Drive
Tallahassee FL 32301
850-922-6007
850-488-0366 (fax)

Tate's Hell State Forest
1621 Highway 98 East
Carabelle FL 32322
850-697-3734
850-697-2892 (fax)

**Three Rivers State
Recreation Area**
7908 Three Rivers Park Road
Sneads FL 32460
850-482-9006

**Tiger Creek Preserve
The Nature Conservancy**
225 East Stuart Avenue
Lake Wales FL 33853
863-678-1551

Tomoka State Park
2099 North Beach Street
Ormond Beach FL 32174
904-676-4050
904-676-4060 (fax)

**Topsail Hill State Reserve
Gregory E. Moore RV Resort**
7525 West Scenic Highway 30A
Santa Rosa Beach FL 32459
850-267-0299
850-267-9014 (fax)

Torreya State Park
HC2 Box 70
Bristol FL 32321
850-643-2674
850-643-2987 (fax)

Tosohatchee State Reserve
3365 Taylor Creek Road
Christmas FL 32708
407-568-5893
407-568-1704 (fax)

Turkey Lake Park
3401 Hiwassee Rd
Orlando FL 32825

Twin Rivers State Forest
7620 133d Road
Live Oak FL 32060
904-208-1460
904-208-1465 (fax)

Upper Tampa Bay Trail
Ranger Station
813-264-8512

Van Fleet State Trail
12549 State Park Drive
Clermont FL 34711
352-394-2280
352-394-1318 (fax)

**Volusia County Parks and
Recreation**
123 West Indiana Ave
Deland FL 32720
904-322-5133

Wakulla Springs State Park
1 Spring Drive
Wakulla Springs FL 32305
850-922-3632
850-561-7251 (fax)

**Wekiwa Springs State Park
Rock Springs Run State Preserve**
1800 Wekiwa Circle
Apopka FL 32712
407-884-2009
407-884-2014 (fax)

Welaka State Forest
PO Box 174
Welaka FL 32193
904-467-2388
904-467-2740 (fax)

West Orange Rail Trail
455 East Plant Street
Winter Garden FL 34787
407-634-5144

**Withlacoochee River Park
Pasco County Parks and
Recreation**
4111 Land O' Lakes Boulevard
Land O' Lakes FL 34639
813-929-1260
813-929-1258 (fax)

Withlacoochee State Forest
15019 Broad Street
Brooksville FL 34601
352-754-6896
352-844-2356 (fax)

Withlacoochee State Trail
12549 State Park Drive
Clermont FL 34711
352-394-2280
352-394-1318 (fax)

FLORIDA'S HABITATS

Many recreational users of Florida's natural places have a desire to know something about the habitats they are visiting. This interest seems to grow as people spend more time in Florida's great outdoors. It is hoped that the following information will help recreationists identify the natural systems around them.

The words "ecosystem" and "habitat" are often used interchangeably in scientific literature. In this ecologically aware era, the word ecosystem is often mentioned. It refers to the way plants and animals relate to each other and to the environment.

The following are habitats a visitor to Florida's natural recreational places might encounter.

DRY PRAIRIE
Florida's dry prairies are grass-dominated and lack trees. Dry praires are like pine flatwoods, but without the trees. The phrase "wet prairie" is confusing, as it does not refer to prairie at all, but to a type of marsh. Even a dry prairie can become wet in certain seasons.

Best Examples. The best examples of dry prairies included in this book are found at Kissimmee Praire State Preserve and Myakka Prairie, a Sothwest Florida Water management District land adjacent to and managed by Myakka State Park.

DUNE
There is no desert in Florida. Dune in Florida usually means a coastal dune. The different dune areas are often described as upper beach, fore-dune, back dune, and inland. Different plants are associated with these areas of the dunes, and with the dunes in different regions of Florida.

Best Examples. The best examples of dune systems included in this book are found on barrier islands. In Northwest Florida, spetacular dunes exist at St. George Island State Park, St. Josephs Peninsula State Park, St. Vincent Island National Wildlife Refuge, and along many portions of Gulf Islands National Seashore. On the Atlantic Coast, great dune systems are found along the barrier islands on highway A1A. Guana River State Park is one of the most prominent locations.

FRESHWATER MARSH
Marshes are wetlands that differ from swamps because they are dominated by grasses, not trees. Swamps are also wetlands, but are dominated by trees.

Best Examples. The St. Johns River has its headwaters in marsh systems in Central Florida. This is in the area around Blue Cypress Lake and Fort Drum Marsh. The central system of the Everglades is a very large marsh historically created by the overflow from Lake Okeechobee. Other interesting marsh areas include portions of Big Cypress National Preserve in South

Florida, and Emeralda Marsh, included in the North Florida section of this book.

HARDWOOD FOREST
Temperate hardwood forests are dominated by trees other than pine. They are frequently called "hammocks" in Florida. In extreme South Florida and the Keys, they are called tropical hardwood hammocks because many of the trees are tropical in origin.

Best Examples. San Felasco Hammock State Preserve near Gainesville is the most diverse hardwood hammock in Florida. Tropical hardwood hammock can be found in Collier-Seminole State Park.

SANDHILL (or HIGH PINE)
The names sandhill and high pine have the same meaning. They are high, well-drained areas, predominately covered with longleaf pine and drought-tolerant oaks, and as such are prime land for housing development.

Best Examples. Sandhill is most widely found in the Central, North, and Northwest regions. Apalachicola Bluffs and Ravines and Torreya State Park have excellent sandhill areas. Many places, however, have sandhill. Others include Gold Head Branch State Park and Wekiwa Springs State Park.

MANGROVE
This type of system is dominated by mangroves, an imprecise term which applies to a group of similar trees that live at the edge of saltwater. In Florida, there are four unrelated species of "mangrove:" black mangrove, buttonwood, red mangrove, and white mangrove. The range of mangrove extends into Central Florida. Mangrove is not found in Northwest Florida, nor in the northernmost reaches of North Florida.

Best Examples. Mangrove in the so-called Ten Thousand Islands begins at Collier-Seminole State Park and stretches far south into the fringes of the Everglades. Many smaller islands on the west coast, such as Weedon Island, also have mangrove.

MARITIME FOREST
Inland vegetation on coastal uplands varies widely. Forests on the coastal dunes are called maritime, and can include palms, pines, oaks, and other trees and plants.

Best Examples. The wild Gulf side of St. Vincents National Wildlife Refuge has spectacular dunes adorned with maritime forest. Some forests in Talbot GeoPark are also maritime.

PINE FLATWOODS
Woods dominated by pines on poorly drained soil is known as pine flatwoods. This is the most extensive habitat on land in Florida. Humans have harvested the trees almost everywhere this habitat is found in the state. Pine flatwoods

barely extend into South Florida, but is found widely in all the other regions.

Best Examples. Many of the areas in the Central, North, and Northwest regions of this book have flatwoods to some extent. Some of Florida's finest flatwoods are in forests, both national and state. The largest forest in Florida is Apalachicola National forest. Ochlockonee River State Park has some especially beautiful flatwoods.

SALT MARSH
Like freshwater marsh, this habitat is dominated by grasses and herbaceaous plants.

Best Examples. Saltwater marshes are numerous along Florida's coastlines. Some scenic areas include Lower Suwannee and Cedar Keys National Wildlife Refuge on the Gulf Coast, and Merrit Island National Wildlife Refuge and Canaveral National Seashore on the Atlantic Coast.

SCRUB
Scrub is usually found on excessively dry and sandy soil. Scrub can be identified by what grows on it. Since Florida rosemary, scrub oak, and sand pine are often found in this habitat, they are useful as "markers" which help in identification. Scrub is found inland on ridges, pariculary the Central Ridge, and in some coastal areas.

Best Examples. Central Ridge scrub is spectacular at Lake Wales Ridge State Forest. Other favored scrub areas include Catfish Creek State Preserve, also in Central Florida. Some of the most northern interior scrub is found at Camp Blanding and Gold Head Branch State Park. Coastal scrub is found along the beaches in many places in Northwest Florida, including Ft. George Island State Park. The largest sand pine forest in the world, the Big Scrub, is located in Ocala National Forest.

SOUTH FLORIDA ROCKLAND
This habitat is found in the limestone areas of South Florida. Both pine and hardwoods grow on rockland. Hardwoods are trees other than cypress, pine, red cedar, and white cedar. The hardwoods grow in isolated hammocks.

Best Examples. Portions of Big Cypress National Preserve and Everglades National Park have this habitat.

SWAMP
Swamps are wetlands dominated by trees. They are often named for the predominant tree. For example, a cypress swamp.

Best Examples. Swamps are found throughout the Florida mainland. Two of the most well-known and remarkable are Corkscrew Swamp Sanctuary, managed by the Audubon Society, and Fakahatchee Strand State Preserve. Many locations in this book have swamp in their inventory of ecosystems.

INDEX